Writing About Reading

From Book Talk to Literary Essays, Grades 3–8

Janet Angelillo

HEINEMANN
Portsmouth, NH

To
Lucy Calkins,
whose teaching changed my life forever

Heinemann

361 Hanover Street
Portsmouth, NH 03801–3912
www.heinemann.com

Offices and agents throughout the world

Library of Congress Cataloging-in-Publication Data
Angelillo, Janet.
    Writing about reading : from book talk to literary essays, grades 3–8
/ Janet Angelillo.
        p. cm.
    Includes bibliographical references
    ISBN 0-325-00578-8 (alk. paper)
    1. English language—Composition and excercises—Study and teaching
(Elementary).   2. Language arts (Elementary).   3. Reader-response criticism—
Study and teaching (Elementary).   4. Report writing—Study and teaching
(Elementary).   I. Title.

LB1576.C31795 2003

372.62'3—dc21   2003014223

Editor: Kate Montgomery
Production editor: Sonja S. Chapman
Cover design: Suzanne Heiser, Night & Day Design
Cover photo: Joel Brown
Compositor: Laura Proietti, Argosy
Manufacturing: Steve Bernier

Printed in the United States of America on acid-free paper
12 11 10 09   RRD 10 9

Contents

Foreword

Sometimes I feel like these are difficult days in which to live out a reading life.

As I write this, it is April 2003 and the war in Iraq seems to be coming to an end. The actual physical war, that is. The war of words we've waged around it for months now, I suspect, will go on and on. And I believe that it should. I believe in the necessity of words, words that represent many different opinions and ideas, to help us find our way in times like these. It's just that I feel exhausted sometimes trying to think my way through all these words. Every news story, every feature article, every editorial asks that I question its source, its motive, question even its particular choices of words to describe the events that unfold.

So I lose myself in fiction.

Fiction. That wonderful genre where writers so generously serve us up a story and say, "Go ahead, enjoy! Not a bit of it is true." And I want to believe this. Sometimes I go to fiction searching for a world where I don't have to ask a single question. But it never happens. I go through page after page of *The Corrections* and on every one, all I want to do is scream at Jonathan Franzen. "How could you make me enjoy this when I can't stand even a single one of your characters?" I invest *weeks* of my life waiting to find out what happens to Sugar, the heroine of Michel Faber's *The Crimson Petal and the White*. Eight hundred and thirty-three pages later, the story ends with no resolution, only a curt goodbye from our narrator, "An abrupt parting, I know, but that's the way it always is, isn't it?" People should be locked up for ending an 833-page book that way.

So it's gone lately with my reading life.

Right in the midst of feeling a little worn down by all my reading, I received Janet Angelillo's manuscript for *Writing About Reading: From Book Talk to Literary Essays, Grades 3–8*. From the very start, I longed to go back in time and be a child in one of the classrooms Janet writes about. In the very first chapter Janet says, "It is powerful for children to realize that they don't have to accept everything that is written on the page, that they have a responsibility as thinkers to question and make meaning from their reading." And it is powerful, but it only continues to be empowering if a reader knows how to *manage* all that thinking and questioning. That's what so many of us didn't learn in school, and I know that's what leads me to feel overwhelmed sometimes as a reader.

In this wonderful book, Janet takes us into classrooms and shows us children who are thinking and questioning and having rich conversations in response to their reading. In clear, consistent ways, she helps us understand how these children are learning to use a variety of tools and strategies to help them harness their ideas as they read through texts, and how they are supported with lots of teaching which helps guide them on the journey as they think their way through a text.

What sets *Writing About Reading* apart, however, is that Janet shows us how to move children beyond the rich conversations and unpolished writing they do to capture their thinking, and into clear, articulate *writing* about their thinking about reading. And what valuable work this is. How many of us adults rant on and on about something, but if asked, "Could you put that in writing?" we feel paralyzed at the thought? We didn't leave school feeling confident in that way about writing about our thinking. It's one thing for me to be so angry at a Bill O'Reilly editorial that I have trouble breathing; it's quite another for me to settle down, figure out exactly why I'm so angry, and write a letter to the editor in response that explains my thinking.

Janet's book helps us envision classrooms where students are taught to do just this—to formalize their thinking in specific ways and then communicate that thinking in a kind of writing that actually exists in the world of writing. I believe this attention to real-world genre is another real strength of the book. Janet takes all our best thinking about genre study and uses it to help us frame curriculum for writing about reading—to write book reviews, first read and study how book reviews are written; to write author profiles, first read and study how author profiles are written. . . .

In the final chapter Janet says, "Our best teaching requires that we raise the bar for students so they do the very best work with the books they read, not the minimum." I believe that in writing this book, *she* has raised the bar for *us* as teachers. The students we teach today are reading their way through a world so full of information, ideas, stories, opinions—a world so full of words—we must teach them in ways that help them make their way through it with confidence. Reading Janet's book helped me realize that these don't *have* to be difficult times in which to live out a reading life, not if we feel strong and ready as readers. Through our teaching, may we grant strength and readiness to the children of today.

—Katie Wood Ray

Acknowledgments

I cannot recall the first, nor even the fortieth, time that Lucy Calkins has said just the right words to me. So many times she has seared my heart with her brilliance and stirred my mind. So many times she has seen with clarity and discernment through situations I thought were hopeless. So many times she has lifted the level of my teaching and filled me with joy in this profession we have chosen.

I thank Lucy for the chance to work beside her at the Teachers College Reading and Writing Project, the opportunity to meet every Thursday with her and her staff, and the chance to grow new ideas and reexamine old ones. Along with Lucy, the project staff helped me think about this book, and I thank all of them. It is impossible to know where my thinking ends and theirs begins, so in many ways, the entire Reading and Writing Project staff is alive on these pages. I especially thank my dear friend, co-director Laurie Pessah, who takes phone calls and questions at all times of the night and day. Senior staff developer Carl Anderson, who was once my staff developer, had insights and suggestions for major revisions at every step of the way. Isoke Nia, whose stance in life is that there is some way to make your thinking sharper and smarter every day, made an enormous impact on my thinking. Deputy-director Kathleen Tolan pushed my thinking about teaching reading workshop in ways that surprise and energize me even to this day. Gaby Layden, Mary Ann Colbert, and Leah Mermelstein always supported me with their wisdom and strength. Paula Marron, Jane Bean-Folkes, and Rob Ross took the ideas to classrooms and returned with feedback from teachers and students.

Our work always stands on the shoulders of those who have come before us, as Lucy says. None of my thinking stands apart from the many writers in the field of literacy, especially Randy Bomer, professor at the University of Texas and NCTE president-elect, and Katherine Bomer, authors of *For a Better World*. All of Katie Wood Ray's work is foundational for my thinking. I always hear Katie's voice in my mind, asking me, "How will you make your teaching smarter?" I thank them all for every opportunity I've had to talk to them.

It is impossible to name all the teachers with whom I shared these ideas over the course of more than a year, but I am grateful to each and every one for their input. My thanks also go to the many teachers who actually helped me research, including the members of my Leadership Group: Carolyn Castagna, Danielle Cione, Dana Dillon, Kathleen Estes-Milano, Minette Junkins, Aliza Kushner, Mary Lauritano, Marilyn Lopez, Scott Nourok, and Robert Ross. A special thank-you goes to another fine group of Leadership teachers: Sarah Daunis, Elizabeth Iadavaia, Helen Jurios, Joanne Kelleher, Lori Marr, Jennifer Naccash-Chan, Barbara Rosenblum, Robyn Scher, and Ruth Stanislaus. I thank the numerous teachers in and around New York City who contributed to my thinking: Reva Schneider of PS 94 in Queens, Christine Bluestein and Sarah Colmaire of PS 199 in Manhattan; Connie Wu, Karen Perepeluk, Maria Iams, and Barbara Rossi of PS 59 in Manhattan; Meredith Serota and Miranda Milledge of PS 116 in Manhattan; Mary Ellen Lehner, Kathy O'Hare, Darren Wittko, Abby Devaney, Jennifer Orsi, and Danielle Bemonte of Bethel Middle School in Bethel, CT; and Deborah Scofield and Lisa Schofield of Dows Lane School, and Kerry Moscato of Irvington Middle School in Irvington, New York. I am also grateful to the principals and assistant principals of these schools for supporting my work and for always doing the best for students: Leslie Zackman of PS 59, Ann Marie Carillo of PS 116, Carol Stock of PS 199, Irma Marzan of PS 165, all in Manhattan; Dolores Garcia-Blocker of Dows Lane School and Lauren Allen of Irvington Middle School in Irvington, NY; Patricia Cosentino of Berry School, Brian Kirmil of Rockwell School, and Stephanie Rypka of Bethel Middle School in Bethel, CT; and Ann Paulsen of PS 21 in Queens, NY. In the end, it is impossible to name everyone I met who contributed their insights and thoughts to this book.

Of course, I thank my editor at Heinemann, Kate Montgomery, for all her patience and prodding. She kept me going with her wise words and clear, global vision. I am grateful for her work on my behalf and for her integrity and friendship. There were many times when she helped me figure out what I really meant to say.

I also thank my dear friends at Chappaqua Meeting, for keeping me in their hearts and thoughts, and Shirley McPhillips, Carl Anderson, and Charles and Cheryl Angelillo, who read the manuscript at various stages and gave me invaluable feedback. Thanks also to Mark Angelillo and Alex Smith for their technical support.

Finally, no one knows more vividly how a writer lives than her family, and it's clear to me that writing a book takes a whole family. First, a writer needs someone who acts as the "glue," so my thanks to Charles, who held things together while I sat at the computer and ignored the dogs, the dinner, and the phone for hours on end. A writer also needs someone who entices her away from the computer sometimes, so thanks to my children, Cheryl, Mark, and Alex, for making me laugh and play every day. And there are those who simply require the writer's love, so thanks to my animal friends, who sometimes sat on the keyboard to get my attention, but who mostly waited patiently for mom to run with them. Okay, guys, let's go.

You Have to Have an Idea

L ate January cold blew in the windows as a group of students huddled in my seventh-grade classroom. Earlier they had found a box in the closet with back copies of *Horn Book* magazine and *Riverbank Review*, and they gathered in my room at lunch to pore over the magazines. As I puttered around and changed a bulletin board, I overheard their conversation.

"Look at this! A review of *Walk Two Moons*! We just read that!"

"What'd they say? Did they like it?"

"Oh, my gosh! An interview with Gary Paulsen! I love this guy's books!"

It was an all too rare sight: five adolescent boys and girls all choosing to spend lunch reading reviews of their favorite books, making comments about whether or not they agreed with the reviewers, and marking longer essays they wanted to read at home. Finally, at the end of lunch period, one student, Liz, said to me, "Hey, Mrs. A., why were you keeping this stuff secret?"

Secret? Yes, indeed, why had I kept them "secret"? Why hadn't I made all my resources for reading about books available to my students? Why hadn't it occurred to me that, as literate students, they would want to read authentic writing about books? I read book reviews, commentaries, literary essays, and author interviews all the time—why shouldn't they?

It occurred to me that day that there was more to my students' engagement with the *Horn Book* and *Riverbank Review* than the legitimacy of reading published texts. What they read in the magazines was written with authority, as if experts on each book were advising others about it. Yet my students rarely if ever read each other's writing about books, and they rarely wrote with a sense of authority or had something original to say about a text. In fact, I am ashamed to admit, their writing was intended for me, their teacher, and after they noted their grades, all of it went forgotten into writing folders. All those papers just filed away in darkness. All that thinking left unshared and unread by eyes other than my own.

I met with those students the next day. What could we do to get some of that excitement from reading reviews into our own writing about books? They were filled with ideas: we could have a magazine of book reviews or put them into a database for the school; we could start a book club or online chat room for talking about books; we could write blurbs for books to advertise them; we could write to newspapers about issues and refer to books we'd read. The energy about this was so different from their usual middle-school malaise. It was as if they understood instinctively that this type of writing really mattered because it would go out into the real world of the class, the school, and the community to be read by others and to affect their reading lives. So the idea was born: they would write in real-world genres of writing about reading, and their writing would be read by many people, not just their English teacher. And, as Lucy Calkins says, since the best way to teach children to write about literature is to teach them to write literature, we would teach them to write well, so that they'd be proud to send their writing into the world.

Writing About Reading All Year

One of the first things I did after this was look at my curriculum plan for the year. I noticed immediately that there was no space in my writing instruction for teaching children how to write about reading. I had fallen into the trap of asking them to write about their reading without teaching them how to do it. I knew that I had to spend some time studying the genres I decided to teach and that I had a lot to learn about how reviewers and essayists write these genres. In fact, I realized that there was so much embedded in each of these genres that I could teach writing about reading all year.

This is not to suggest that all a teacher would do all year long in writing instruction is writing about reading. Nor would we only teach writing about reading at reading time. On the contrary, there is much other work to be done during both instructional periods. There is writing work to teach, including studying other genres, teaching qualities of good writing, mastering written conventions, and so on. And there is reading work, the many strategies children must learn to be efficient readers, including decoding and other basic interactions with print. But there is a symbiotic relationship between reading and writing instruction (Harwayne, 1992) that teachers can emphasize at some times during the year and that fit quite well when teaching writing about reading.

How the Year Might Go

A year of teaching writing about reading needs to be carefully planned. Because so much of what students will be writing comes from the conversations they have, you'll want to spend time early in the year getting children to talk about books (Britton, 1993; Berthoff, 1981). One way to do this is to read aloud to them every day, using that read-aloud time to model the ways to think and talk about books (see Chapter Two). Much of their early conversation will be based on the read-aloud book. By October, they should be in partnerships (Calkins, 2001) where they are regularly meeting to talk with another student about texts they are reading, and by November, you should be pushing them to take notes of various kinds from their reading and conversations. At the same time, you should introduce the concept of a readers notebook (see Chapter Four) as a way to record thinking and conversation and to plan for longer pieces of writing. Much of this work is done during reading instruction, because it is part of reading, thinking, and talking about books. When children have their readers notebooks established, you'll want to teach some of the possible genres of writing about reading. This will be part of writing instruction, even though they will be writing about information from their reading. Your teaching will focus on how to write this genre, using the notes they took while reading and talking about their books. In this way, instruction in both reading and writing complement each other.

The units of study in actual genres of writing about reading will usually come after the holiday break or the fourth month of school, as it will take a few months to teach them to think while reading, take notes to prepare for conversations, talk with others, take more notes based on conversations, and then reflect on these notes. You will not be able to teach all these genres, but whatever you do teach should become part of the expected writing in the room from that point on. Some schools might decide to plan vertically, with students learning different genres in different grades. But whatever you decide, it is vital that students understand they are being taught how to write these genres so they can then go out and do it again and again, each time they have something to say about a book. Working to teach students that readers write about the texts that affect them will not happen until there is a paradigm shift. The focus of writing about reading must shift away from students writing to prove something to us. If we release students from the tyranny of book reports or the triviality of mobiles as responses to books, we must replace those "activities" with work that is meaningful. We want them to know that writing about reading is serious business. When we ask them to respond in cute, mundane, or repetitive ways, we communicate something to them: we communicate that responding to books is cute, silly, or boring.

Learning to respond powerfully to books is one of the great truths they will learn in school. It reflects their thinking and their learning lives. It takes many forms because it is so complex, as their learning lives should be. And it cannot be taught in one unit of three or four weeks, because it is too vital to their learning.

What You Need to Get Started

One thing we'll examine is the role of conversation in getting students to think clearly and thoroughly about texts, but for this to occur, you'll need to establish a certain atmosphere in the room, a safe environment where students know they will be encouraged and respected (Peterson, 1992). Children learn best in an atmosphere where they feel they can speak and question freely and exchange ideas without being in "social danger." Teachers can encourage this by modeling and establishing routines for conversation and by creating an atmosphere of calm acceptance and unbiased confidence in students' abilities. In whole-class and small-group conversations, students need their thoughts to be valued and supported, while at the same time the teacher scaffolds their thinking for clarity and text evidence.

You will need some clear structures in the room before beginning to teach writing about reading. One is the basic structure of organizing your teaching into whole-group, small-group, and individual instruction (Calkins, 2001). You'll also want to set up a system for assessing your students to ascertain their needs, both as readers and as writers. This needs assessment will help drive some of your instruction as you tailor your units of study to the needs of your students.

Students will also need materials if they are to read and write. I prefer well-stocked classroom libraries filled with outstanding books that are matched to students' levels, but I realize this is merely a dream for some schools. Some schools use a combination of trade books and a fine anthology. Even if students are working from an anthology, it would be wise to have as many books as possible available to them for independent reading. Children will also need a notebook in which to record their responses (see Chapter Four) and adhesive notes or index cards. Other materials, such as colored pens and highlighters, are useful but hardly necessary for students to do good work. Teachers may find chart paper or an overhead projector and blank transparencies helpful for demonstration. Beyond this, tools for assessment, systems for note-taking about individual students (Anderson, 2000), and an ever-expanding knowledge of children's literature are essential, as well.

So this is how the work to prepare for writing about reading might look in September:

❖ assess students and fit them with books they can read

❖ begin reading aloud regularly

❖ use the read-aloud books to spark discussions

❖ carefully scaffold students toward accountable talk, that is, including everyone in the conversation, staying on topic, keeping with the text, and so on

❖ give students chances to talk in small groups about the read-aloud text

❖ occasionally model jotting down on chart paper some of the points made in the conversations

❖ ask students what they would write down from the class conversations if they were keeping notes; write these on a chart for later reference and to show how notes look

From the very first day of school, teachers can be laying the groundwork for students' thinking and talking about books that will set the stage for later writing about reading.

Schedules and Timetables

A year of writing about reading has to start with reading. Whether students are reading books on their levels (Calkins, 2001; Fountas and Pinnell, 1996) or in a student anthology, they must know that reading is one of the most important things they will do in school. They must spend a significant amount of time reading every day in class, in addition to whatever reading they might do at home. Frankly, reading is just too important to be solely an "at home" activity. And teachers will want to be learning about their students as readers and writers during the first few weeks of school, as well as establishing a safe learning community. This is a good time to get children reading, sit with them to assess their reading, and begin to read aloud to them every day. It is unlikely that children will be ready to produce long writing about reading yet. (Any review of summer reading should be kept to conversations in small groups, rather than writing reports or taking tests.) Figure 1–1 shows one teacher's plan for reading and for writing about reading across the whole year.

The most important message we can give to students is that reading and writing matter so much that we will find time for them every day. And every day there will be some kind of instruction about and practice of reading and writing skills, not just assigning pages to read or papers to write.

Schools where the schedule allows at least forty-five minutes for each are giving a solid literacy foundation to children. A forty-five-minute period for reading or writing might consist of ten minutes of direct instruction, followed by independent work while the teacher works with small groups or individuals, followed by some wrap-up or sharing of their work. In schools where these blocks are not scheduled, teachers must do whatever they can to provide reading and writing time for children or to lobby for changes in future schedules.

In the remainder of this chapter, we'll look at some ways to get started and how to use reading aloud to teach thinking skills early in the year.

Showing Students the Pleasures of Reading a Good Book

One of the first things teachers must do, before we can ever ask children to write meaningfully about their reading, is to reveal to them the pleasures of reading a good book and the fun of recognizing a "bad" one. It is powerful for children to realize that they don't have to accept everything that is written on the page, that they have a responsibility as thinkers to question and make meaning from their reading. Louise M. Rosenblatt (1995) tells us that all reading is a transaction between the reader and the text, that the reader's job is to make meaning of the words on the page and to take an active stance while reading. It seems logical to think that if the reader is interacting with text and using his or her intellect to make the text come alive, the experience of reading will be more meaningful and enjoyable.

Once we can get children to comprehend and respond thoughtfully to texts in conversation and in short jottings to record their thinking, we can then work on the muscles of writing well in authentic genres of writing about reading. But we should not expect that children will be able to do the writing work until we have heavily scaffolded their thinking and note-taking, as well as their organizing and planning of their writing. Using reading aloud, partnership reading, and supported independent reading, we can teach children to think about books in meaningful ways and to write about them from the thoughts they produce in conversation.

What the Students Should Be Able to Do by January and June in the Fourth Grade

SEPTEMBER

Unit of Study Building stamina and meaning
Big Idea(s) Accumulate the text
Strategies Ask questions; gather information about the setting, characters, and plot as the story unfolds; retell
Writing About Reading Jot on Post-its

OCTOBER

Unit of Study How stories go: folktales, fairy tales, and myths
Big Idea(s) Anticipating
Strategies Talk longer off the text; create mental images; look out for problems/obstacles and anticipate resolutions; reread
Writing About Reading Writing off Post-its

NOVEMBER

Unit of Study Talking, thinking, and writing about reading 1+2 (whole-class study on friendship and independent work)
Big Idea(s) Having ideas about the text
Strategies Look out for cause and effect connections; reread; find evidence to support ideas/theories
Writing About Reading Chart with argument from their point of view; write longer responses; pick three best Post-its and then write a reflection/response

DECEMBER

Unit of Study Nonfiction reading
Big Idea(s) Developing theories
Strategies Think about character motivation; create webs; infer what is not directly said
Writing About Reading Write a summary of a book(s)—three sentences? *or* write a book report

JANUARY

Unit of Study Close reading of short texts
Big Idea(s) Writing for the ELA
Strategies Make comparisons; infer; question what an author is saying or has left out; integrate ideas across parts of a text
Writing About Reading Write a persuasive commentary with an angle and evidence *or* write about literary text they've read (either would have a thesis or a point of view/angle and information to support thesis)

FEBRUARY

Unit of Study Thinking and talking across texts—book clubs (whole-class genre)
Big Idea(s) Revising thinking
Strategies Listen to peers and reread texts; find evidence to support new ideas; integrate ideas across texts or parts of a text; have new ideas and develop new theories
Writing About Reading Write three related paragraphs—a comparison based upon an issue

MARCH

Unit of Study Social action book clubs
Big Idea(s) Locating ideas into the world
Strategies Research; infer what is not directly being said; have ideas and develop theories; integrate ideas across texts
Writing About Reading Write a persuasive essay to educate or create change

APRIL

Unit of Study Reading within a thematic study
Big Idea(s) Thinking about an author's message, big idea, or lesson
Strategies Develop theories; find evidence to support ideas; infer what is not directly said; differentiate sources; integrate ideas across parts of a text(s); research
Writing About Reading Write a letter to the author *or* an author profile

MAY

Unit of Study Reading–writing connections
Big Idea(s) Thinking about and studying a variety of genres (including literary essays)
Strategies Study different genres of writing; review books read; name issues that came up in books read and in reading log; research
Writing About Reading Create a list of what a literary essay is comprised of *and* write in different genres

JUNE

Unit of Study Reading projects
Big Idea(s) Bringing it all together—writing a literary essay
Strategies Use reading logs to find books on subject, etc.; skim reading notebooks, looking back at notes taken; use evidence from each book to support theory
Writing About Reading Write a literary essay on three to four books

FIG. 1–1 *Teacher's year-long plan for reading and writing about reading*

In this chapter, we will look at some ways teachers can open up reading enjoyment for children, while showing them ways to think about and interact with books. I first encountered the idea of "thinking aloud" when I read Katie Ray's book *Wondrous Words* (1999). Teachers can model their thinking for children while stopping and musing aloud during the read-aloud time. As teachers will be reading aloud to children every day, perhaps several times a day, they can use the read-aloud to teach many things, not the least of which is how readers think and talk about books.

One of the first places we can begin to shape students' ways of thinking about texts is by using the read-aloud time to model ways to think. What we carefully and explicitly teach them to do through the read-aloud will become the things they do in their independent and partnership reading. Therefore, we'll look first at ways to use the read-aloud to our best teaching advantage, as we give children containers for the ways they can consider and talk about the books they read.

◈ reading aloud to create shared conversations

◈ reading aloud to model types of thinking

◈ reading aloud as a springboard for new thoughts

Reading Aloud to Create Shared Conversations

It was a warm September day, and Rob Ross sat on a chair in the rugged meeting area of his fifth-grade classroom. His students sat around him, some of them sprawled on their backs, others cross-legged, and some on small benches. Rob was reading aloud from *Holes* by Louis Sachar, a book he had read to his previous class and had become a cornerstone of their classroom conversation. *Holes* is the story of a boy who is falsely accused and convicted of a crime and sent to a juvenile prison where the warden requires inmates to dig holes every day in the blistering sun. Rob finished reading Chapter One and looked up.

"Well, what do you think?" he asked, looking around expectantly.

There was no response. Nothing. Just a sea of empty faces. Finally Hatesh raised his hand and said, "It was nice."

Rob's mouth fell open. "Nice? Hatesh, tell us what you mean by *nice*."

Hatesh shrugged. "You know. Nice. Good."

Rob shook his head. "Okay, we need to talk about this. I can't imagine that all of you would just sit there and hear this chapter and have nothing to say about it."

Diana raised her hand. "It's just good to hear you read to us."

"Yes, I know that. It is good to be read to. Thanks for being brave enough to say that, Diana. But I need you all to think while I'm reading. I need you to have a thought about the book, to be ready to say something about it to a neighbor, to a friend, or to me. That's what good readers and good listeners do. They are always using their minds to take what they are hearing and to make some meaning from it. It's more like playing video games than watching TV. With TV you can just zone out, but with video games, you've got to be involved. And you've got to be involved with books."

Then Rob read the chapter again and modeled his thinking by stopping and saying it aloud as he read. He told the class that of the many things he was thinking, some of them were things he would want to talk about with other people. Some of his thoughts were just questions about the text, for example, how could there be no lake at a place named Camp Green Lake? But other thoughts were deeper and fuller, and he jotted them down on a chart for the class to see.

"These fuller thoughts are ideas I think I could talk about with other people for a long time," Rob explained. "But I could also use my questions about the text as ways to get some talking going. So my question about there being no lake at Camp Green Lake could get some conversation going about how clues like that build expectations for us as readers. We already know from the first sentence that there is something very wrong with this place."

Rob's class helped him make a chart of what he was thinking. Later, they went back and named what they were thinking so they could try to reproduce it in their own thinking about text. The chart looked like this:

Part of the Book	What I'm Thinking
No lake at Camp Green Lake.	The author wants me to see that things are not as they appear.
No town left here; weather is too hot.	This is a forbidden place. Why is there a camp here?
The Warden "owns" the shade.	How can someone own shade?
Rattlesnakes and scorpions don't bite. Usually.	What happens to you if they do?
Why are campers digging holes by the no-lake?	Are they looking for water? Why would they make you dig holes in the heat? Isn't that child abuse?
What is a yellow-spotted lizard?	I may have to look this up in a reptile book.
Who would want to go to a camp like this?	I wouldn't send my daughter there. What kind of parents would send their child there?

Rob's students were fascinated. "You did all that thinking in two pages?" Matthew asked.

"Yes," Rob said. "And I know you can do it, too."

The next day Rob went on to read Chapter Two. First he told the class that he was expecting them to think as he read to them and that he would give them time to think and time to talk. Rob was using Judith Langer's framework of stop and think, stop and talk, stop and sketch. He knew he would eventually ask the children to stop and talk, but for now he was content to get them thinking. Rob knew that the only way to get children to write meaningfully about what they read was to have them think meaningfully first. So as he reread the last few lines from Chapter One to remind them of the plot, he asked them to stop and think for a minute. At first, the class seemed uncomfortable—the teacher was not asking them questions about the book, nor was he "testing" them on comprehension—but they quickly realized that Rob just wanted them to think about what he had read to them. The children all appeared to be ready to hear more of the story. Rob later told me he was willing to accept almost anything reasonable the students said that day, just to get them to respond to the book. He knew that once he assessed what his students already knew about responding to books, he could scaffold their thinking to be deeper and more insightful.

Chapter Two of *Holes* is very short. But it clears up some of the questions in the reader's mind about Camp Green Lake, and it poses some interesting ideas. One idea is that some people thought that digging a hole every day in the hot sun would turn a bad boy into a good boy (page 5). When Rob paused in his reading aloud and asked the class to say something about that, most of the students erupted into indignant responses.

"That's not fair," Jameel said. "They could die in the sun. Who were the people that thought that was the right thing to do to them?"

"Having to dig holes in the sun would only make you angry, not good," Melissa said.

"I'd be meaner and badder than ever after that," Joey said.

Rob smiled. It was clear they were responding to the book and that some interesting conversation was beginning. Rob continued to read the page and then asked students to stop and think about the end of the chapter. Then he asked them to go off with their partners and talk about what they were thinking. He went around the room eavesdropping on some conversations and taking notes on his notepad. Then he called the class back together.

"Okay, I heard people say some very smart things. Let me tell you some of them. Then we'll give what you do a name, so you can do it again."

Diana stood by the chart paper to take Rob's notes down.

"I heard one partnership talking about the idea that some people have certain ideas about what is good for others and that often those ideas can be really mean or wrong. Let's think of a way to name that."

The class thought for a minute. "Let's call it 'thinking about the opinions people have'," suggested Nyal.

"Good," Rob said. "Here's another one: The choice the judge gave Stanley wasn't a choice at all. Let's name that."

"'Things are not always what they seem'?" Molly said. Diana wrote that on the chart.

"Okay. The last group I listened to said that Stanley was tricked into going there because he was poor and he didn't know what real camp should be like. What do you think?"

Desmond raised his hand. "I think that proves he's stupid. I've never been to camp, but I know it's not a place where you dig holes, and I know that if they sent you there instead of jail, it's got to be bad."

Diana added Desmond's thinking to the list.

Rob smiled. "This proves to me that all of you can think. All of you can have thoughts as we are reading a book together or as you are reading a book alone. All of you can push yourselves to figure out a story or any text. Today I want you to try to push yourselves to have at least one thought about your independent reading book and to be ready to share that thought with your partner. Some of the ideas in the second column of our chart might give you an idea of what you can think about as you read your book."

Chart of Partnership Thinking About *Holes*

Event from the Book	What We Think About It—Book Ideas
Some people think they know what is good for others—the judge thought it would be good for Stanley to go to Camp Green Lake, and warden thought it was good to dig holes.	People's opinions can affect others, especially if they are powerful people.
Going to camp or jail wasn't a choice at all.	Sometimes things don't go the way you would like them to and things aren't as they appear to be.
Stanley was poor, so they took advantage of him.	The world can be an unfair place.

The chart gave students some specific events to think about, as well as ideas about how to grow those events into bigger conversations. Again, Rob was not concerned in this first read-aloud with the quality of their ideas, although he would not have allowed them to consider any ideas that were totally unfounded in the text. He knew there was much more he could and would teach them in the weeks ahead about thinking and talking about books. What's important here is that Rob used his own thinking about a text to model for students what he wanted them to do. Then he showed them how to go from an observation about an event to a more global statement. These global statements would provide ways that children could begin to think about their own books.

Reading Aloud to Model Types of Thinking

Within a week, most of Rob's students had the concept that you had to have an idea as you read. They were regularly talking about the read-aloud book, *Holes*, and they were trying out the same strategies (stop and think, stop and jot, stop and talk) in their independent reading books. They also had the idea that you could look for certain bigger ideas, such as "things are not always what they appear to be" in many books. But Rob noticed that students seemed to get on one type of thinking, such as asking questions, so he decided to use the read-aloud again to model types of thinking.

After reading aloud from Chapter Ten of the book, Rob removed the adhesive notes he had written from the book. He read them to the class and asked the students to classify them.

"Here I wrote that I feel how much pain Stanley is in and I know how he must ache because after I play softball I sometimes feel like that. What can we call that?"

Diana raised her hand. "'Feeling like the character'?"

"Good. Let's get that down." He wrote that on the chart next to his adhesive note.

"This one says that Stanley thinks he found a way out because he found the fossilized fish. I think he's getting greedy."

Hatesh raised his hand. "That's 'character motivation.' It's about why Stanley did what he did."

Rob continued. "And this one says that *Armpit* is a bizarre name."

Ibrahim answered. "That's 'looking for clues or noticing details.'"

Eventually the class made a chart with different types of thinking that they could do in the books they were reading, as well as in the read-aloud book. The items on the chart could provide them with things to think about as they read and ways to prepare for conversations with each other, just as the previous chart helped make their literal observations more global.

Some Early Types of Thinking About a Book

◈ empathy for a character

◈ trying to understand a character's motivations

◈ noticing details and wondering what they might mean

◈ thinking about the significance of unusual names

◈ thinking about how the world in the book affects the character or the story

◈ questioning what's happening in the story and what doesn't fit

◈ wondering where the story will go next

◈ information I must get to understand this story

◈ thinking about fairness in the story

Armed with the above list, the students went off to read their books and prepare for conversations about them. Some of the partnerships were reading the same book, in which case the conversations could go very deep into the book. Others were reading different books, and their conversations needed to focus on more abstract ideas and on pointing out places in the text where each partner could show examples of what he or she was thinking. In any case, it was now clear to the students that they were reading for more than getting the literal meaning of the words on the page and that they were capable of thinking about stories in deeper ways. Rob's modeling also gave students specific things to look for as they read, such as needing more information to understand or noticing a detail that doesn't fit with the story and wondering why it's there.

Reading Aloud as a Springboard for New Thoughts

Marilyn Lopez was a fourth-grade teacher in Rob Ross' school. She heard what Rob was doing with his class and decided to visit during her prep period to watch and learn. She was so excited by what she saw and heard that she went back to her room to try it with her own class. After doing the same things with the read-aloud in her room, *Crash* by Jerry Spinelli, Marilyn decided to see if she could teach her students to go beyond the text and to grow new ideas. She also wanted to push them to write important things on their adhesive notes, because she felt many of the adhesive notes were wasted with written remarks such as "wow" and "yes." Although Marilyn didn't want her students to write long paragraphs on their adhesive notes, she felt that the tools should be used to their best advantage. She wanted to teach students that although notes are short, they must mark some insight or thinking rather than a passing thought. She also noted to herself that later in the year she would work more on the difference between interesting and important information.

After Marilyn read *Crash* to them, she constructed with the class a chart of types of thinking that was similar to Rob's chart. But she wanted them to go even further. Marilyn had read Randy and Katherine Bomer's book *For a Better World* (2001), and she hoped that much of the reading could be put into a framework for social action or, at least, for social awareness. So where children had listed *empathy* as one way to consider a text, Marilyn extended it to consider the action one could take based on one's "empathy" for a character.

In *Crash*, the main character, Crash Coogan, is an antihero, a young man who is a star athlete but whose cruelty toward others earns him a reputation and eventually some retribution. Spinelli wrote the book as a window into the heart of an athlete, but there are other layers to this book. Marilyn's class took on the cause of the underdog, that is, the character of Penn Webb, who is tormented by Crash because he is a naïve, gentle soul and a Quaker. He also seems to have everything Crash really wants, such as a family and love. Following are the issues the class brought up as they read through this book, although their chart looked different from Rob's because they focused on the issues first and then the events in the text.

What We're Thinking About in *Crash*

◈ Why are some people singled out because of their religion? Why did Spinelli make Penn a Quaker, not a Catholic or a Jew? Did he think he would offend the fewest numbers of people by making him a Quaker or did he really need Penn to be a Quaker in the book? Do we need to know more about what Quakers believe to figure this out? Should we think about Penn as Every-Religion, so we don't make fun of anyone because of their beliefs? How should we treat anyone who is different in any way? Do we see any injustice around us in the ways kids are treated in this school, and what can we do about it?

- ❧ Why do some people act mean toward others for no apparent reason? Why do people hate each other? Should we accept that some people are like this, or can we hope that people can change? If we think people can change, what can we do to help them? What can we do when we see kids being mean in the schoolyard or cafeteria?

- ❧ What does it mean to be unselfish? Is anyone really capable of being totally unselfish? Do you ever see anyone around you acting like this, or have you noticed times when people could have been unselfish or kinder, but weren't?

Marilyn's students were developing more abstract ideas because of her willingness to model her thinking and to discuss larger issues, or themes, in books. Her assumption was that the students would understand the book on a literal level, because she was reading aloud. To be sure, she put a system in place for those who were having difficulty, but otherwise assumed all children were capable of talking about the book.

The students broke into small groups based on the large question from the chart that they wanted to discuss. They took notes on their conversation so they would be able to report back to the large group. Then they took their notes and spread them out to look for categories or threads of thinking. Finally, Marilyn asked them to summarize their talk about at

---

Helping Children with Literal Comprehension

Realistically, some children struggle with literal comprehension. There can be many reasons for this, including struggling to understand a complicated plot or missing a cue to a change in time or setting. Some structures you can set in place to help these children are:

Ask partners to retell stories to one another. Teach them to listen for places where the story doesn't make sense or there are holes that affect their understanding, and stop their partners. Teach them to say things like: "Can you tell me that again?" "I'm not sure what happened there." "Tell me that part over."

Show them how rereading the first chapter of a book can help them get the "setup" of a book and put them on their way to understanding the rest of the book.

Have them stop at the end of each page for a comprehension check, always asking themselves if it makes sense.

Show them how it looks when you understand a book (you'll have to be an actor here!), using facial expressions to show confusion and understanding. Then teach them to monitor themselves for the first signs of breakdown in understanding, so they go back and reread before reading without comprehension for too many pages.

---

least one of the questions in a paragraph to hand in to her. Although she felt the students had had a good introduction to finding a social awareness idea, thinking and talking about it and finally using notes to summarize, she knew she would come back to this work again later and build on it to support longer and deeper writing.

Teaching children to see literature this way, in a larger context, shows them that books are more than stories; they are doors into knowing ways to live and be in the world.

Summary

Before we can ask children to write about reading in meaningful ways, we must teach them to think about reading in meaningful ways. By modeling your own thinking during your read-aloud, charting, and naming the kinds of thinking, you can give children frameworks for thinking about books, which will lead to deeper, more interesting writing. If their thoughts are dull, their writing will be, too. If they are excited about the ideas they can extract from books, they will be more likely to produce interesting, well-thought-out writing. Most importantly, we must remember to carefully scaffold conversations so that children will gradually come to know that deep talk about a book is something they can all do.

Producing Thinking About Books in Preparation for Writing

- Model aloud the thinking that you are doing about your read-aloud book. You can begin with a shorter text, such as a picture book or an editorial, and then move to a longer text, such as a chapter book.

- Ask students to be ready to say, sketch, think, or write something during your read-aloud times. Stop at regular intervals to allow them to do this. Listen to what they are saying and scaffold their learning by highlighting insights for others.

- Let them practice doing this regularly. Ask them to go off with a partner and talk for a long time about their thinking. One way to do this is to refer back to the text for evidence, so they can talk together with the text close at hand, pointing to examples from the book to support their thinking.

- Ask children to choose one thing to talk about and stay with it for a long time. Often in a group, children will each say their ideas in turn and then think they are done. Choosing and staying with one idea for fifteen minutes will force them to grow new thinking about it, rather than flitting from the surface of one idea to another, without deepening any thinking.

◈ Teach children to capture some of the smartest things they said on an adhesive note. Have them put the adhesive notes in their independent reading books or tape them in their readers notebooks for later reference.

◈ Name the kinds of thinking (questioning the text, wondering why something happened) that are going on in the room and chart them. (See Chapter Two.)

◈ Chart the ideas that groups of children are studying. Add the names of children, as well as specific examples from the read-aloud books. Regularly ask each group how their thinking is going.

◈ Assess how students are doing (from literal comprehension to coordinating talk) and plan for small-group or individual work accordingly.

Thinking and Talking About Texts in Read-Aloud and Partnership Conversations

When actors or musicians rehearse for a performance, they go over their material many times, trying it this way and that, looking to discover beauty and truth in a score or script, seeking to uncover meaning, and working to interpret their texts. Artists know that performance comes only after thinking, rethinking, interpreting, rehearsing, working out rough spots, getting more information, talking to others, studying previous performances—in short, after lots of practice. They know that most of the work for a performance comes before they actually perform.

If we consider that writing about reading is in some way a performance where students show how they have interacted with and used a text to make meaning, it is essential that we give them time to prepare for performance. Students must be taught to "rehearse" for their writing by thinking and talking about texts, by examining texts in this way and that, rethinking, negotiating, and debating with themselves and others. Teachers can think of themselves as directors or conductors, responsible for the integrity of the performance, but providing room for students to think as individuals and make meaning from all they read.

Unfortunately, many children don't know what to say about a book beyond "I liked it," or "My favorite part was. . . ," so we must teach them how to talk about books and give them visions of what they can actually say. Our direct teaching must provide frameworks for children to understand that there is much more to reading a book than naming favorite parts. We must teach them that books are, as James Britton (1993) tells us, a source of experience about the world.

Ellen Keene and Susan Zimmerman (1997) write about teaching children to make connections, ask questions, and use sensory images as windows to comprehension. And surely these are ways in which children can begin to glimpse the depth we want them to experience in a text, particularly if we push children to use these strategies wisely. All too often students are content with surface work that gestures toward deeper thinking but does not extract their best thinking. Deeper thinking flows from some change, friction, or discomfort that leans against what we already know or believe. Good readers make space for opening their minds to print, allowing ideas in, and then situating the new ideas within the old, making sense of a text in comparison to what they already knew about the world. Interpretation expands as we merge what we know and think with the experience of reading words in a new text.

How do we teach kids to do this, especially when some of them struggle just to read the words? Before we begin, it is best to follow the wise instructions of Lucy Calkins (2001), Irene Fountas and Gay Su Pinnell (1996, 1999, 2001), Stephen Krashen (1993), and others: Children must read books on their levels, and they must read comprehensible texts. It is only by reading books they can understand that children will become better readers. It is as much folly to expect children to read books that are too hard as it is to ask a novice pianist to play Chopin études. When children are reading texts appropriate to their levels, they are ready to start to do all the interpretation work we want and need them to do. And if they are reading texts they can understand, we can teach them to talk, think, and take written notes in preparation for later writing.

Based on this objective of teaching them to think, talk, and take notes about texts, you might identify several categories for your fall teaching:

◈ teaching the content of what to say when talking about books

◈ teaching strategies for remembering conversations, insights, evidence, questions, and jotting down notes about these

◈ teaching how and when to use jots, charts, or longer nonnarrative writing to track information and/or thinking in a book

◈ teaching rereading notes purposefully and using them to plan longer pieces of writing

Teaching the Content of What to Say When Talking About Books

Mary Ellen Lehner teaches sixth grade in Connecticut. She established read-aloud time early in the school year and the expectation that children would think and respond to the texts she shared. But she noticed that several students sat quietly during read-aloud talk time. Although Mary Ellen stopped several times during the read-aloud for students to talk to a partner or talk in small groups, a few children held back and refused to participate. When Mary Ellen asked why, they dropped their eyes and shrugged their shoulders. Yet they appeared to be engaged when Mary Ellen read, and they could answer direct questions about the text.

Mary Ellen finally figured out that these children, who were new to the school and had not been in reading workshops before, just didn't know what to say. Their talk strategies were limited to mentioning unfamiliar vocabulary, retelling favorite parts, and then waiting for the next teacher directive. Mary Ellen decided to work with them on a curriculum of "talk content," that is, what someone actually says about a book, as well as the social conventions of keeping a conversation going.

This is important because without the content of what to say, students will not know what to write when the time comes. If they haven't had practice coming up with and rolling ideas around in conversation, it will be difficult for them to handle writing their ideas later. We must carefully scaffold students' learning each step of the way so they are supported and they clearly understand what we want them to do. Furthermore, we must model how to do it for them. Telling them to "say more" is merely a directive, not a strategy for how to do it. If we avoid teaching children how to talk, it will be no surprise when students later write, "I have nothing to say" or "I don't have a favorite part" or "This book was nice." Explicit teaching will produce explicit talking, which will eventually produce explicit writing about texts.

Mary Ellen brought her students to their meeting area and began teaching them what they could talk about in book conversations. Following Katie Ray's ideas for constructing curriculum from one's own life (2002), Mary Ellen carefully noted the kinds of things she heard people say about books in her own book club, in printed reviews, and on the radio. These things became a long list of ways that literate people think and talk (and eventually write) about books and became the basis for a curriculum of talk (Figure 2–1). Mary Ellen's focus was on exploring ideas about books through conversation, not on point-by-point retelling, which

Ways to Think, Talk, and Write About Books

- having hunches about the text, the story, the author, and the characters

- noting places in the text that don't ring true and wondering why

- setting the text beside one's experience or knowledge to help comprehension

- noting turns or twists in the plot or in a character's attitudes or actions and using that to build understanding or a theory

- finding places in the text where a light goes on in my mind and signals me to pay attention

- making larger observations about how this story illuminates life, or the nature of good and evil, or ideas about honesty, beauty, truth, and justice

- rereading that brought new understanding or insights and why; noting how a second reading changes my perception of a text

- identifying archetypal characters or plots in the book and using them to aid comprehension

- using what I know about genre to help me read and think about character, plot, and theme

- making connections to important literature I know, for example, fairy tales, myths, legends, or other books in my own personal "canon" of books I know and love

- noting that this story seems too obvious, so rereading and digging deeper

- identifying possible imagery in the book and how it unfolds

- making notes for discussion with other readers of the book or previous readers; planning for ways I will feed my reading social life with this book

- citing the text to confirm my ideas or reshape them

- identifying story elements and how they help the reader understand the story

- writing down important or pivotal quotes from the text and reflecting on them—writing off a "telling line"

- bringing who I am and what I know about life to my understanding of this book; recognizing that sometimes this biases the reading of a text

- recognizing that I need to get some additional information before I can understand this book because it is so foreign to my experience

- reading with a critical stance to help me understand the book; appreciating style and craft

- finding literary, movie, or television allusions in the book

- finding an idea thread to follow throughout the text or building a theory about the text

- noting the tone and atmosphere and how they affect my reading

- finding places where a text disappoints me and wondering why

- finding places where a text surprises me or takes an unexpected turn

- questioning the point of view in the story or thinking about how it broadens or limits the story

- observing gender roles or portrayals of families and minorities

- recording places where I have allowed myself to be changed by literature or where I have resisted change and "argued" with the author

FIG. 2–1 *Ways to teach children to think, talk, and write about literature*

is in itself a valuable skill, but not in this context of growing thoughts about texts.

After the class had practiced choosing items from the chart to talk about, Mary Ellen decided to emphasize one item that she thought would produce fertile conversation. She wanted students to think about books in terms of characters and to have lots of ways to talk about characters. So again through the read-aloud book, she modeled her thinking about the characters and let the students practice doing that, too. She could easily have chosen plot or any other category, but she knew her children and knew that characters would yield lots of good conversation for them.

Mary Ellen's work shows how teachers must be reflective about their teaching and must assess their students daily to determine exactly what to teach. Based on what they needed, she decided to teach them the content of what to say, but she could have gone in another direction instead. Seventh-grade teachers Abby Devaney and Kathy O'Hare felt their students knew what to talk about but didn't know how to talk. The children seemed to think a conversation was each person saying his idea in turn, with no attempt to bounce any ideas back and forth. So the teachers devised a series of lessons in which they taught children how to have a conversation about the read-aloud texts and the ways people move conversations along.

One strength of the read-aloud structure lies in the support it gives children as they go off to talk about their partnership books. In the fall, you'll probably want to establish book partnerships for children, where the partners are reading the same title. This structure provides students with the support of another reader to help with the reading, as well as a chance to practice the talk strategies the teacher is modeling. Students can take the same strategy demonstrated in the read-aloud and do it with their partners. They quickly try the strategy with the read-aloud book during the active engagement part of the minilesson and then go off to do it with their partnership books. For example, if the teacher used the read-aloud to demonstrate what she did when the text confused her, children would then have one concrete strategy for something to do when confused in a text. This kind of demonstration and guided practice provides careful, gentle scaffolding for sophisticated work.

It is important to remember that the reason for talking is to prepare children for taking notes and that taking notes will prepare them for longer writing about reading. That is why you'll want students' conversations to become rich with ideas and why you'll want to teach them to begin to take notes on what they say and hear in these talks.

Teaching Strategies for Remembering Conversations, Insights, Evidence, Questions, and Jotting Down Notes

Barbara Rosenblum taught her third graders that adhesive notes and notebooks were wonderful places to capture good thinking from book conversations and to develop this thinking into writing over time. She knew that eventually she wanted them to write about their books, so the notes they took of their conversations could provide them with many ideas for longer writing. Her third graders said insightful things during their read-aloud and partnership conversations, but she worried about the quality of their jottings. Although students stopped to take notes on adhesive notes during the read-aloud and while reading their partnership books, their written notes lacked the depth and originality of their oral remarks.

"If they can't capture their thinking in jots and little notes, how will they ever recall the smart things they are saying?" she lamented. "And if they can't remember the ideas they developed in conversations, how will they write about their reading with insight and authority?"

Barbara understands that the quality of conversation directly influences the quality of student writing. But she also understands that many children can't get their ideas down on paper. Perhaps writing is too laborious for them, or they stumble over complete sentences, or they just don't know what is important to write down. Whatever the reasons, and I'm sure they differ for different children, the jottings often aren't effective for documenting or recording conversations.

Watching children, you can see how hard it is for many of them to write. First they have to find their adhesive notes, then they have to sharpen their pencils, and, finally, they must work hard to use their best penmanship so the teacher can read it. By the time they start to write, they've forgotten the smart things they wanted to say; they've muddled it with worrying about how to begin, how to spell it right, or how to say it in full sentences. By the time they start to write, they have nothing left to say.

One thing you can do is to teach children that taking notes looks different from writing a paragraph. No one expects notes to be in full sentences or to begin with capitals or to be neat (although obviously they must be legible). When we bog down children with these requirements, they are unable to capture their thinking, and it is lost. How often have we heard students say things that are so insightful, yet what they end up writing is mundane at best, far from their animated ideas in conversation. So teach children by modeling for them that note-taking looks very different from other writing; it is short, quick, and efficient. (Figure 2–2).

Another thing to try is asking partners to help each other remember what was said in conversation. I've paired up two partnerships and assigned one group as scribes for the other. So if Mark and Mary are partners and Sam and Sandy are partners, Mark will listen for and write down what Sam says, and Mary will do the same for Sandy. Then the partners

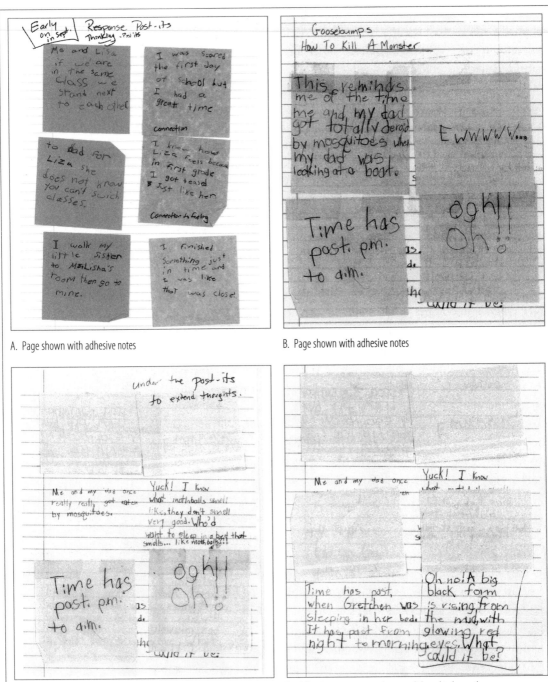

A. Page shown with adhesive notes

B. Page shown with adhesive notes

C. Adhesive notes removed to reveal thoughts beneath

D. Adhesive notes removed to reveal thoughts beneath

FIG. 2–2 *Sample of Response Notes*

can switch. In the end, each student gets the gift of her words written on adhesive notes to put into her book or her readers notebook. Often children are surprised and exclaim, "I said that?" but they are pleased to have their words in writing.

When it is too hard for children to write fast enough to record talking, you can tape-record their conversations. Then they can play back what they said, and stop the tape to write down the things they want to remember. This is not as laborious as it seems, because their conversations are not that long and there may be only a few things that need to be recorded. I would certainly model this for children so they would see how to do it.

Teaching How and When to Use Jots to Track Information or Thinking in a Book

Sometimes the information collected on adhesive notes is just too much for the size of the note. There are times when children will need to move away from adhesive notes and use time lines, charts, or other organizers to help them track their information. In general, I would tell a child who is finding examples of something on every page that she needs to record that information on something other than adhesive notes, such as a chart in her readers notebook. There may be occasions when a student wants to copy quotes from a book as evidence for some line of thinking she is following. Again, this might be best done in the notebook or on some other larger sheet of paper. Adhesive notes are not only expensive, they are also small, and students should record only small bits of information on them.

Aliza Kushner told her fourth graders that there needed to be a limit to the number of adhesive notes they could use in a book. She was reluctant to set a number, but she told them that at the beginning of a book, when they were just getting their ideas going, it was okay to use more adhesive notes, but that once they were on a line of thinking and were collecting evidence, the work might transfer to their reader's notebooks, where a chart might be a better place for recording. She did this because she found children with books where every page was plastered with so many adhesive notes that the print was not visible! Although Aliza was thrilled that her students had noticed so much on every page of their texts, she knew that some of it was "sticky-madness" and was not high-quality work. She felt she needed to refine her students' use of the tool.

Knowing when and how to use a tool is an important skill. I have seen students who think they must fill out every graphic organizer they have ever encountered before they can write. Clearly these children do not understand the purposes for graphic organizers, just as Aliza's children were misinterpreting the purposes of adhesive notes. Especially as we consider that the reason for most note-taking is to produce longer pieces of writing later, we must emphasize that lots of random adhesive notes do not prove that a reader is practicing qualities of good reading at all. Getting and staying on a line of thinking throughout a book is more important than accumulating adhesive notes.

You might deliberately teach this to students by actually modeling the note-taking you would do from a read-aloud text. Let them see the brevity of the notes, as well as talking about why you made the decision to take each note. Students must see that you've chosen key words, not full sentences, that you've used abbreviations for characters' names, and that sometimes you forego taking a note on something that is interesting but is not important. Show this to them again and again, and talk through it, letting them practice note-taking from the read-aloud by talking their decisions over with their partners before actually writing anything down. Knowing what to write down is a sophisticated skill—in fact, many of us know adults who can't do it and still highlight every line on a page. It is best to let students practice frequently during the read-alouds. Then quickly assess how they are doing and send them off to actually take notes on their books. Use the information to plan small-group or individual instruction and to plan subsequent lessons on strategies for effective note-taking.

Sometimes students will need longer phrases, sentences, or short paragraphs to record their ideas or conversations. Again, you'll want to demonstrate this for them, as well as why you chose to do this. In fact, students must understand that there is not one type of note-taking that will serve every purpose: an adhesive note cannot do what a T-chart can accomplish, and a web doesn't capture the cohesiveness of a paragraph. But each of these is appropriate for its purpose, and children should have a repertoire of these tools available to them and the freedom to choose which one to use.

Rereading Notes and Using Them for Longer Pieces of Writing

For some books, the notes a student produces may be all the writing you'll require. These notes should be clear and organized and demonstrate how a student's reading of the text progressed or how his thinking grew. However, there will be just as many times when you'll ask students to write more, whether it's a response of a page or two, a book review, or a literary essay. Clearly, children will not be ready to write essays if they have not taken notes and used those notes to extend their thinking into a longer written response. By the third month of school, you'll want to nudge children toward doing this.

Helen Jurios pulled beside one of her fifth-grade students for a reading conference. "Tell me about the reading work you're doing today, Krishma," she said.

"Well, I just finished my book and I have all these adhesive notes in it. And I'm wondering what to do with them now," Krishma said.

Helen smiled. "That's a good question, because it shows me that you are thinking about having purposes behind everything you do. It's not about putting tons of adhesive notes in your book, but about using those adhesive notes to do some work."

Helen asked Krishma to go back and reread every adhesive note in her book, looking for one adhesive note that she wanted to think and say more about. As Krishma did this, Helen conferred with other students and noticed that others were confused about the purposes for writing adhesive notes. So she decided on a string of minilessons for the students on ways to use your notes to get longer thinking. Here is the first minilesson she did.

Helen's Minilesson on One Way to Write off an Adhesive Note

CONNECTION "Yesterday I noticed that some of you were having trouble deciding what to do with all the adhesive notes in your books when you were finished reading. I told some of you to reread them, but I know you had some trouble making sense of that. So today I would like to show you one thing you can look for when you reread the adhesive notes you've put into a book."

TEACHING "First, let's look at some of the adhesive notes I wrote about the book I just read, *Coraline* by Neil Gaiman. I put them on a transparency for you to see. When I reread them, I see that some of them are more interesting than others. For example, look at this one. It says, "bored—needs ways to amuse herself." That one surprises me, because it seems like I was judging Coraline in my mind as I was reading the book. So I want to think and write about that one a little more. I think I have more to say about it, or more to figure out about what I was thinking as I read that book. Watch while I make some notes on my page about what I'm thinking about that adhesive note and the book." [Helen writes a reflection on the transparency.]

ACTIVE ENGAGEMENT "Right now, could you look through your book and find one adhesive note you think you can say more about? Then turn to your partner and talk for two minutes about it." [The class does this while Helen goes around listening to them.]

OFF YOU GO "That was good work. I heard some of you saying you weren't sure why you had written an adhesive note and you needed to reread the book to figure it out, and I heard someone say that her best adhesive notes were the ones with the questions on them. Today during reading workshop, I'd like you to reread your adhesive notes again. This time, I'd like you to look for an adhesive note that surprises or confuses you or where you wrote something that you think you could explore more. Talk about the adhesive note with your partner to see if you can get yourself to do more thinking. Then take that adhesive note and put it in your reading notebook. If there is time, do some writing about it."

This strategy of rereading one's notes, whether on adhesive notes or in a notebook, is crucial. Often children take notes and never look at them again. They move on to the next assignment or next chart to fill out and completely forget that the notes are there to help them further their thinking. Obviously, notes are essential when preparing to write, but at this stage, children have just been preparing to talk. Helen wanted her children to know that they could mine their own notes for thinking and that sometimes there are gems among the mundane. In fact, she wanted them to know that there needs to be both kinds of notes: the brilliant, knock-your-socks-off thinking ones and the ones that simply track and record evidence of that thinking. She also wanted them to know that she would be expecting them at some point to be able to produce longer writing about some of the adhesive notes, so that the quality needed to improve.

The next day, Helen called the class together again. In her conferences the previous day, she had seen students picking adhesive notes randomly, and she wanted to shape the way they were choosing. Her minilesson for the day was on choosing the adhesive note, thinking and talking about it, and then writing an entry in their notebooks about it. She modeled what she meant by writing her own entry on an overhead transparency and then

Early Assessment of Writing About Reading W...

Early in the year, your purpose is to teach children to think and talk well and to ?
ing and from their conversations. Therefore, you want to assess how well student·
ments can be based on notes you take as you listen to students' conversations, ⌐ ⌐
what they say (literal versus some inference, showing comprehension of the book versus confu·.
to identify some ideas to talk about in the book and so on), as well as the way they conduct the conversations (bouncing an idea around before abandoning it, taking something and growing it as an idea, helping each other to build understanding, inviting quiet members to talk). Once they begin to take notes, you'll
want to look at these notes to assess the quality of their thinking (surface skimming or insightful) and
whether they are learning to capture some of what they say onto paper. You'll also want to assess how
well they are using the tools (for examples, sentences on adhesive notes versus using charts for stretching
ideas) and making decisions about what information or insights to write down and whether to use short
notes or charts or go to longer responses. Finally, you might ask students to hand in their notes for evaluation. Younger children might choose their best adhesive note to hand in; older children could choose their
five best adhesive notes, put them on a sheet of paper, and then write a paragraph about how the adhesive notes relate to one idea or trace the growth of an idea. Each child chooses which of his notes he
wants to be evaluated, and you will begin to build an understanding of the child as a reader and writer as
you study his notes and conversations. Most important, your daily, on-going assessment through observation and small-group and individual instruction will give you much information to plan your curriculum and
evaluate student progress.

clarifying that the adhesive note she chose must contain some mystery or potential for exploration in talking and writing, not necessarily just because it was about a favorite part of the book. The writing could be in the form of a list, a paragraph, or some ruminating freewriting. The form mattered less than the student's attempt to squeeze more thinking out of the notes. Helen's students went off and produced some very rudimentary, but definitely longer, writing in their readers notebooks.

Summary

The notes children take on adhesive notes, index cards, or small pieces of paper are, in fact, all the writing about reading that they will do about some texts. However, eventually they'll need to write longer pieces about some of the texts they read. You will want to show children that within their notes there are surely some ideas that they can explore further in longer responses. At first, these longer responses can be oral, as they talk to you or their partners about their notes. But in a short while, you'll want your students to reread their notes and be able to stretch their thinking to write longer. How long this is will obviously depend upon the ages of the students; younger children may only write half a page for a longer response, while older children will push themselves to write at least a page. Before we can ask students to attempt a book review or literary essay, we must scaffold their thinking so they can expand ideas through conversation and through exploratory writing. Next I'll examine some concrete ways to teach students to do this.

Teaching Children to Jot Notes and Write Short Responses

- ❖ Set the stage by listening to student conversations and telling them that you hear so many wonderful things you wish you had written down.

- ❖ Using the read-aloud book, model notes you would take (on a chart or transparency) from the text; be sure to say why you chose to write something down.

- ❖ Listen to their partnership conversations and/or their "talk group" conversations (Chapter One) and model notes you would take from those, including why you would write some things down and not others.

- ❖ Show children how notes should look (single words, short phrases, abbreviations).

- ❖ Demonstrate rereading lots of small notes, seeing some connection between them, and organizing them into a chart.

- ❖ Teach children that there is a reason behind taking short notes versus writing a chart.

- ❖ Take a short note or chart that you made from the read-aloud and demonstrate writing a longer response from it.

Literary Thinking Across Texts

In the last chapter I looked at some ways for students to begin talking and thinking about books together. The mental workout of a good conversation has so many benefits for all students, not the least of which is the feel-good sense of a satisfying talk with others. This experience also offers children who struggle with reading texts the chance to see that they can still think, talk, and jot about books, because the support of their community helps them, even when reading printed words or extracting meaning is frustrating. I believe all readers can think, talk, and write about books if they have scaffolding and some frameworks to follow, regardless of the level at which they are reading. Although this work is important for reading, in terms of writing about reading it can prove invaluable, because it shows them they have many things they can write.

Following the initial unit of study in reading workshop where we have assessed readers and matched them with "just-right" books (Calkins, 2001; Fountas and Pinnell, 2000), we can begin to teach children to grow strong in thinking about reading in a second unit of study that focuses on thinking and talking about books. Remember that it is important to initiate the thinking work for writing about reading in the reading workshop, where we will use read-aloud and short shared texts to model ways to think about books.

In this chapter, I will look at some specific ways teachers can model moving toward the higher-order thinking we want students to do and to produce in their writing. This work follows the initial conversations and jottings that were discussed in the previous chapter. That work should be done in September, after you have assessed readers, matched them with books on their levels, established partnerships for independent reading and read-aloud conversations, and set up the routines and rituals for reading. (At the same time, you are setting up the routines and rituals for writing workshop, but the "writing about reading" piece is still situated in reading workshop at this time of the year.) Presumably, students are ready to move forward when you feel most students are comfortable in their books and are meeting with partners to talk about the literal meanings of texts. Then you can teach them some new ideas for thinking about books. These ways include:

◈ making connections that support comprehension

◈ using landmark texts to ground thinking about literature

◈ practicing literary allusion—"name-dropping"

◈ using one's literary history to think about books

◈ thinking about types of plots and characters in books to aid comprehension and talk

Teaching Children to Make Connections That Support Comprehension

In their book, *Mosaic of Thought* (1997), Ellin Keene and Susan Zimmerman write about teaching students to make three kinds of connections. Keene and Zimmerman call them "text to self," "text to text," and "text to the world." These ideas are excellent for getting children to understand ways a reader can connect to books, but equally important is teaching children that the connections must matter to them. Connections that do not help a reader access meaning in a text or that do not expand a reader's understanding are not worthwhile connections. Sadly we all have heard children make connections that are irrelevant to the story—"Oh, the boy has boots; I have boots, too."

One reason I believe children do this is that they do not know how connections "go." They think they are saying just what the teacher wants to hear, because in their minds they are making connections. Obviously, they have not grasped that connections should help the reader get inside the text or into the character's mind, or to feel the emotion in the story. Modeling for children exactly what we mean by connections really helps to clear up these misconceptions. (Figure 3–1). Children may still make inappropriate connections, but at least they'll have something to work toward.

The suggestions in Figure 3–1 all focus on making connections that will help children understand the text and find meaning in what they have read.

Ways to Model Personal Connections to Text

Connecting to an event in the book by asking oneself: What would I do in that situation? Do I have ethical, religious, or cultural traditions that would influence me and make my response different from or the same as the character's?

Connecting to the character's feelings: When have I felt the same emotion? What did it feel like in my body? How do I react in some situations because of my emotions? Do my emotions sometimes affect the way I respond to others, and where do I see characters doing that in the book?

Connecting to a relationship between two or more characters in the book; connecting to the dynamics of the relationship.

Connecting to an issue, like how divorce or foster care affects children, by drawing on personal experience, or people I know, or stories I have heard, or by imagining myself in that situation; be sure these responses are thoughtful and not easy or stereotypical answers.

Connecting to others' views, especially when they are very different; for example, seeing things from the perspective of someone who is much older (or younger), someone who lived in a different time period, someone from a different race or religion, someone in a different socioeconomic group, someone of the opposite sex, or someone who lives in a very different culture or another part of the world.

Connecting to how other characters react to a character in a book and thinking about how I might react to that character. Do their reactions make sense? Do they tell me something I need to know about them or the character? How can I form cross-connections between several characters or connections if I don't agree with or understand them? That is, how do I disagree with a character responsibly?

Forming opinions based on text evidence, but resisting easy judgments of a character, by saying "I can see how this character did this, even though I would do something different."

Connecting to a theory or hypothesis that I am thinking about and using it to help me read through the book; for example, on every page I am noticing that good friends are loyal to each other and thinking about my best friend, how we are loyal to each other, and what loyalty means in a friendship.

Connecting to a passion in my life, like the idea that dads worry too much, or that it's hard to be a boy and not be athletic.

Noticing roles people play and connecting to the roles I play in my life (student, daughter, teammate, best friend, and so on).

FIG. 3–1 *Modeling personal connections to texts that aid comprehension*

Using Landmark Texts to Ground Literary Thinking

One way to teach students to compare texts—text to text connections, in Keene and Zimmerman (1997)—is to introduce the idea of a "landmark text." You could call it something else, but it really stands for a book that remains in someone's mind long after the last page is read. Many adults will mention books such as *To Kill a Mockingbird* or *Catcher in the Rye* as books they think about often and compare to current books they are reading. In some ways, they feel they were changed as readers and as thinkers by the experience of reading these books.

Pratasha was in the fourth grade when she gave her teacher, Marilyn Lopez, the idea of landmark books. She was talking about her favorite book, *Freak the Mighty*, when she said, "A landmark is something you recognize, something you know that has important meaning for you. It tells you where you are, like the deli on your corner; and sometimes it tells you who you are, like the Statue of Liberty or the Great Wall of China. And if you love one of those things, you compare all the other statues or walls or delis to them. Since I know myself and I understand the world better because of this book, in my mind I compare all other books to it." Wise words from a nine-year-old!

A landmark book is a defining book in a reader's life. After reading a landmark book, the reader is a different person, that is, a person is changed by the experience of reading the book. It often stands out because of theme, plot, or characters, and it can help a reader define who he is, what he believes, and what he thinks about the world. Each person has different landmark books, although there are some books that tend to stand out in many readers' minds. It is important to emphasize that I am not advocating the establishment of a "canon" of children's books that all students must read, but rather helping children find the books that will be meaningful to them. It is not helpful to impose the teacher's ideas about which books qualify as a landmark text, but it is helpful to know each child well and attempt to lead him to books that may make this kind of impact.

Each landmark book is worth reading and writing about on its own and can produce beautiful writing about reading because of student investment in the ideas from the text. But these books also can be used as a way to measure other books. For example, I might think about how the book I am currently reading stands up beside *The Great Gilly Hopkins* or *Roll of Thunder, Hear My Cry*. The concept of landmark books can be a way to teach kids to think and write about other books, and we hope that children will learn to position themselves to be changed and moved by special books. Some children will find their landmark texts through the read-alouds the teacher chooses, and others will find them on their own. Whatever ways children discover them, it is useful to teach that we will be changed by books if we expect to be changed by books.

A landmark book differs from the concept of a touchstone text in several ways, although sometimes the two may overlap. A touchstone text is studied in writing as a way to learn about the craft of writing (Ray, 2002; Calkins, 2001; Fletcher, 1996; Murray, 1996), and it is a text the entire class studies together, not an individual experience. Landmark books stand out because of theme, character, plot, or setting, but they are not necessarily studied for the craft of writing (although they can be). Landmark books are individual choices and stand as beacons for comparing characters and plots in other books and for changing one's view of the world. Touchstone texts may or may not do this, and although touchstones may be deeply loved books, they might not be defining experiences by changing a reader's belief system or understanding of the world. Reading a landmark text leaves the reader a changed person. And reading other books with a landmark book in mind changes the way you read and the way you think about books. For example, I may read *Scarecrow* by Cynthia Rylant to study the lushness of her language, but the story may not change me as a person. Conversely, I may be a new person with different eyes to view the world after reading *The Other Side* by Jacqueline Woodson but I may choose not to study it for craft.

Over time, students' landmark books may change, but that is an expected part of growing as a reader and expanding one's repertoire of books. Teachers can introduce the concept to children by talking about their own landmark books. Some children may already have landmark books even if they don't know what to call them; for example, my daughter Cheryl knew *Good Night Moon* as a landmark text before she began school, and she compared all other books to it, event though she didn't call it a "landmark book." As an adult, she knows and loves the fantasy novels of Robert Jordan and Terry Goodkind, and she compares all other fantasy novels to those. Those are genre-specific landmark texts, but Cheryl can also tell you that she is a changed person after reading *The Between* by Tananarive Due and *Beloved* by Toni Morrison and that the ideas from those books about how humans treat each other are in her mind as she reads others. After reading *Silent Spring* by Rachel Carson, she knew that environmental work was going to be a cornerstone in her life, and she frequently thinks and talks about that book as she continues to read literature about the environment. Children tell us that reading *The Great Gilly Hopkins* has changed them because for some of them it's the first time they read a book where the ending isn't what they'd hoped, or they see foster care in a new light, or the main character is not likeable in an obvious way. As literate adults, we've experienced this on our own; as teachers, we can teach it to our students as a way to look at literature. Part of the challenge is to take children on the journey of recognizing their landmark texts or helping them search for them, but the rewards in conversation and writing are great.

Some ways you might introduce the idea of landmark texts by modeling are:

◈ refer to the books that remain in your mind as a support for early book choice

◈ lay out several books you've read and talk about which ones became landmarks and why

- explain the reason a book changed your life; perhaps you were looking for certain answers at that time in your life or were at a certain juncture and the story or characters fit in

- tell students when you found a book that made you say "Oh!" and that made you look inside and see who you are

- tell them that you learned you could trust certain authors to write well in a way that resonated with you and so you returned to those authors again and again

Whether or not students find a landmark text while they are in your class, you can strengthen their reading by making them aware of it. Of course, a landmark does not always have to mean it changed my life forever; it can also mean it took me to a new level in my reading. For children, "life-changing" might mean the first time they followed an author, the first time they knew they loved a certain genre, or the first time they saw a character like themselves. If we talk to them about the things that are alive in our reading, we elevate the level of their reading and we show them that their job is to find bridges between books and their lives.

When Marilyn and I asked her fourth graders about their landmarks, they said these were some of the criteria they used to figure out if a book was worth calling a landmark book:

- Did it make you feel pain?

- Did it make you cry?

- Did it make you forget misery and laugh or smile?

- Did you want to reread it right away?

- Did you memorize lines you wanted to remember forever?

- Did it change your mind or behavior?

- Was it something you were ready or waiting for?

- Did you feel a sense of loss when you finished the book?

- Did you miss the characters?

With these ideas in their minds, Marilyn's students understood that they should expect that a certain percentage of books will do this for them to one degree or another and that they should read expecting this. They also had a concept that gave them language for expecting more from their

Categories of Ways Readers React to Books

Books I really enjoyed but didn't stay with me for a long time. These may include books that are funny, easy, part of a series, suspenseful, have interesting characters, and so on, but they did not make a lasting impression on me.

Books I remember because the story was good, and it made me think about the people I know or how I live. For example, my cousin is a lot like Amber Brown, or sometimes I feel mean like Crash.

Books that taught me something new, like what life is like for animals on the tundra, some things the explorers did, or how to be vegetarian. This is new information that is interesting but may not necessarily be life-changing. These books can be fiction or nonfiction.

Books that taught me something new, and that new information is vital to my understanding of the world. These books can also be fiction or nonfiction. The important thing is that I must work to fit these books into what I know about the world. For example, if I am reading *Esperanza Rising*, *Homeless Bird*, or *Roll of Thunder, Hear My Cry*, which are all about historic or cultural experiences, I may need to get some information to understand them or do some "figuring out." Or I might read that book on how to be a vegetarian, and it may change me in major ways, because I decide to refuse meat, so I do something with the new knowledge.

Books that changed my life, that made me see life completely differently, that made me become a different person, that changed the way I see other people, or that made me aware of biases I didn't know I had. These are the landmark books.

FIG. 3–2

reading. Ultimately, the class decided that books fell into several categories, which they wrote on a chart.

Teachers might use the categories in Figure 3–2 to start conversations with their students. It might be helpful to make a similar list with your students or, with more experienced children, to look back over their reading histories and sort books by categories to see that different books can be in different categories for different readers.

The insights children discover about themselves as thinkers and readers from embarking on this journey to find landmark texts can help them become sophisticated readers. It can help them know which things pull them into a text, what kinds of books have the most impact on them, and how to use what they know about one book to read through or judge another. It also helps them to know that they don't have to love every book they read; in fact, that it is rare for readers to love every book. They can read for pleasure, or for information and, sometimes, to become a new person.

Some of this work might end up as reading projects for some children (Calkins, 2001). They might form independent discussion groups to share or discuss their landmark books as they find them. Most important for our purposes is that they begin to use some of this thinking to help them think, jot, and, later, write longer about books. It might be interesting to put up a chart to which students can add the titles of landmark books as they find them. For every class, it will be a very individual list and each book on the list is one child's choice, not the result of a "popularity vote" by the class. The list below shows the list by midyear from Marilyn's fourth-grade class, although Marilyn was careful to insist that posting the list did not mean that everyone had to love or read those books.

Our Landmark Books

The Great Gilly Hopkins by Katherine Paterson

Roll of Thunder, Hear My Cry by Mildred Taylor

Holes by Louis Sachar

Bridge to Terabithia by Katherine Paterson

Number the Stars by Lois Lowry

Sun and Spoon by Kevin Henkes

The War with Grandpa by Robert Kimmel Smith

Reva Schneider teaches fifth grade in PS 94 in Queens. She and I had studied the concept of landmarks books together one summer at the Teachers College Reading and Writing Project Summer Institute in Reading. When school started, Reva mentioned the idea of finding land-mark books to her class, because she wanted to tuck the thought into her first unit of study and then teach it later in the year. But when she finished her second read-aloud book, *The War with Grandpa* by Robert Kimmel Smith, she asked her class why they thought she had chosen it. Some said it was clearly about fairness, which was the theme they were studying in their independent books. But one student named Mary said, "Because it's just one of those landmark books." Reva was stunned and asked her why. Mary continued, "It isn't just about fairness. It's about the complicated family stuff that you can really hold on to. Fairness is so simple, but being in a family makes it complicated. And when you remember that, you will think of this book."

Reva said she hadn't mentioned landmark books explicitly since letting the students know in the first week of school that they'd be looking out for them that year. She'd told them that the deeper we read, the more likely we are to find a book that could be a landmark for us. Mary took the suggestion to heart, and it changed the way she listened to Reva's read-alouds and the way she read independently.

Practicing Literary Allusion

Whether or not you choose to introduce the idea of landmark texts, you will want children to understand that what we know and think about books often depends on how they measure against other books we know. In fact, the experience of having read even one book makes reading the next book easier, and reading one book while noticing one facet of it, for example characters, makes it easier to read the next book, because you now know something about characters that you can compare it to.

Helen Jurios told her fifth graders that they would be working on literary name-dropping. She told them that whenever they were talking about the read-aloud or their independent reading books, they should try to mention another book or another character. Helen had been modeling this for a few weeks by tucking these kinds of references into any conversations about books. By the time she actually asked her students to do it, they had a clear idea of what Helen wanted them to do. They were used to hearing phrases like:

That reminds me of when I read . . .

It's just like in that book . . .

That's not something that would happen in . . .

I felt the same way when I read . . .

In addition, she tucked in references to past read-alouds and to books she knew their previous teachers had read aloud to them. She frequently said things like, "Hmm, I wonder what Gilly would do if she were in this book?" or "That's not how friendships worked in *Charlotte's Web*." The difference between this and the landmark books concept was that Helen was drawing from the shared book experiences in the room, rather than nudging students toward their own experiences. She was creating a framework to scaffold the idea that you can find ways to connect and compare many stories, even if the stories appear very different.

It is important to recognize that name-dropping is not an end in itself. Helen's purpose for doing this was to teach children that when you close the pages of a book, you do not consider yourself "done." A book lives on in your life and thinking, and you can recall it as you think and speak about other texts. Literate people frequently do this, and they often refer to books or articles they've read or a story they heard. It is a way that literate people act, and children should be able to do this, too. Later we'll hope that, since they have practiced this orally, children will use this as a way to weave literary allusion into their own thinking and writing about books. We also hope it will raise their consciousness to understand that readers and writers make allusions all the time.

Helen also wanted the students to know that there are some characters that can often be used for comparisons. She often used these names in talking about books, saying things like, "I wonder which ways Andrew in *Frindle* is like Gilly Hopkins, you know, just a kid trying to manipulate adults." Through these references, students could see that you can compare stories even when the plots and characters appear to be very different.

The class made a list of characters they thought they might try to think and talk about when they were reading books, such as Gilly Hopkins and the spider Charlotte. Like the list of landmark texts, this list was specific to this class, and every other class will have its own list.

Older students often are delighted by the idea of literary allusion when they begin to hear quotes in movies and on TV. Recently, several eighth graders were excited to be "in on the joke" when they heard a quote from one of their favorite movies, *Monty Python and the Holy Grail*, in a current hit movie starring a Monty Python actor. They began to weave quotes from songs, poems, video games, Marx Brothers movies, and TV shows into their conversations, practicing the fun of literary allusion. Although clearly they will not yet "get" many of the allusions in literature because of limited experience, they now understand that it is there. Eventually they will get more and more and will find reading them satisfying and writing them great fun.

Using One's Literary History to Think About Books

As I mentioned in the last section, once a child has read one book, reading the next book should be easier. Going through the experience of reading a book makes you wiser for the next time. It's like going to a baseball game—the next time you'll expect everyone to stand after six and a half innings, you'll expect the national anthem, and you'll expect peanuts and hot dogs. I would teach children that they can use what they already know about books to help chart their journey through the books they are currently reading and to help them decide what to write on adhesive notes or in their readers notebooks.

Students should begin to expect certain things when they read. They should know that sometimes a book is a story and sometimes it is a list, even if the list is long and elaborate. If it's a story, then they will need to use all they know about story elements to help them read and understand (Calkins, 2001). They also should begin to think about stories they've read as they read, for example, if I know there is usually some big crisis scene—like the chase scene in movies—then I will be looking for that. If I know there is usually a narrator in a story or a main character that the author wants me to "root for," I can use that to help me understand. And I can use some of that language when I jot things down about my book. Words like *narrator*, *crisis*, and *resolution*, can be taught to students through read-alouds, can be identified in books they've already read, and can be used in their writing about reading to sound very smart and informed.

In one of your read-aloud selections, you might think about introducing these literary terms, even for younger children. As you use these words regularly, children will learn to understand them experientially, just as they learn any other vocabulary that is used often and not taught in isolation. Words have meaning when the become part of our bank of words, so using them, rather than assigning them as dictionary work, will help children to regard them as natural ways to think and talk about books.

In some ways, we might think about doing more to tap into the things that children know well and that are part of their culture today. These things may not be part of our lives, but might offer other types of texts that children know very well and to which they could refer. For example, I might consider including video games, which are not part of my repertoire of entertainment options but which are very alive for many students. Talking with students, I've learned that there are many skills that children develop as they become adept at playing these games, and I am sure cognitive psychologists are studying the benefits or drawbacks of these. Children tell me that there are categories of games, and that one category, called "role-playing," involves becoming part of a story, often a quest of some kind, and living out the hero's destiny. An example of this would be the Final Fantasy series, where a conflict is established at the beginning and a player becomes a character who builds himself up to a powerful warrior. Sometimes the story includes complex political and social climates, and the character/player is responsible for saving the world. What an interactive way to teach children to put themselves in a character's shoes! These games have plots and characters, and children must hone their decision making and responsive skills to advance in the stories. Some children become very adept at this, and asking them to think about the ways the plots or characters in their games compare to printed literature is worth considering. It does involve some research on the teacher's part, but using the plots and

Terms You Might Use to Make Children Familiar with Them	
narrator	main and minor characters
plot	complex and flat characters
point of view	climax or crisis
perspective	style
mood	resolution

names from students' experience may help them to understand complex literary concepts easily.

For some children, you could reference films they might know well, such as the Indiana Jones or Star Wars series, which many children have seen on videotape, or more recent releases, which already have become part of the "film canon" for children, such as the Harry Potter movies. Especially for reluctant or struggling readers, who often have well-developed skills in nonacademic areas, it might make sense to try to connect literature to what they already know well. Either way, it is useful for children to see that they can think across texts to find connections and that thinking this way can make their reading richer and their conversations more interesting. For the teacher, it creates a way to have a shared body of texts to talk about and a shared literary history, while validating children's experiences at home with texts other than the traditional ones in schools. And because we are talking about writing about reading, it provides a way for many children to write about what they read. Children can learn to refer to books they read many years ago, even to texts they heard read aloud as toddlers. Knowing any text well can help a reader access a new text. You might even say that knowing a handful of picture storybooks well is a wonderful way to read and to think, talk, and write about literature.

Thinking About Types of Plots and Characters in Books to Aid Comprehension and Talk

One thing teachers can do to help their students think about stories is to plan a unit on how stories go using folktales, fairy tales, and myths. These stories may be familiar to children, who often only know the Disney version, and they offer an opportunity to tap into the resources of other cultures. The interesting thing is that many of the same types of stories show up again and again in different cultures, under different names. Thus, the trickster in Rumpelstiltskin shows up as Anansi, and in other folktales as well.

These stories often follow similar patterns, such as the ideas of good versus evil, young versus old, immortal versus mortal, and so on, resurfacing in many of them. If you read children some of these stories and point these patterns out, they begin to think of other books that way. Where do they see good versus evil in their books, or the friction between the old and the young, or the tension between immortal/magical creatures and mortal ones? Finding these ideas in Cinderella, Sleeping Beauty, and Snow White is relatively easy for children and can quickly become a way to think about books. Suddenly, they have a way to measure the book they are reading: What would the seven dwarves do? Based on what you know from Cinderella, how do you think this will end?

There also are some universal ideas that surface in myths and folktales. These include the quest or journey to save something vital, the idea of meeting and overcoming obstacles, the opposition of some clever enemy, and the unlikely, gentle hero who finds courage deep within himself. Students will quickly recognize Bilbo Baggins and Harry Potter as types of characters; they will recognize the plot as the way the hero overcomes evil. There are universal themes: good and evil, loyalty and betrayal, sacrifice and selfishness. These themes show up again and again and provide lots of opportunity for students to talk and write about them.

Folktales and fairy tales often contain stock types of characters that help children understand their roles in stories. These include the hero, the antihero, the bully, the wise fool, the elder mentor, the sidekick, and the villain. If we teach these types to children through folktales, they may be able to recognize them in modern books. We hope that this thinking will help them understand that not all characters are the same, that many stories go in similar ways, and that knowing some of the ways stories go can help them build an expectation for how their own reading will go. Although this is helpful as a reading strategy, it also gives students a framework for writing about what they've read.

Sarah Daunis decided to teach her fourth-grade class common story plots using folktales, fairy tales, and myths. She identified four plot types and showed them to her class using folktales and other stories they would know, such as the Star Wars stories. After she talked about the plots and characters, students began to easily identify how other stories might go and to understand that the characters in their books tended to fall into some of the categories she had named for them. Thus, they saw Gilly and Crash as antiheroes, Esperanza in *Esperanza Rising* as a hero and her mother as a wise elder, Winn Dixie as a wise fool, and Phoebe in *Walk Two Moons* as a noble sidekick. Looking at literature this way helped give students containers into which some of the plots and characters fit and gave them more ways to think, talk and later write about books.

**Plot Types and Other Archetypes to
Help Students Think About Their Reading**

Four Possible Plot Types

Romance

wishes come true

goodness triumphs over evil

heroes live happily ever after

journey or quest with minor or ordinary adventures

plot leads to a major struggle, test, or ordeal

quest ends successfully

characters often return to the point where journey began

Tragedy

there are limits to people's ability to make wishes and dreams come true

catastrophe or death of a heroic character

there is a loss of innocence

there is some sacrifice in support of a cause

often leaves us with hope because tragic figure shows highest human
     attributes

Satire and Irony

show the discrepancy between what is and what ought to be

attempt to change people and society for the better

often use ridicule to expose hypocrisy

Comedy

not necessarily humorous

contains a rebirth or renewal after obstacles have been overcome

Archetypal Characters

Archetypal characters often appear in stories and have their foundations
in mythology (for example, the wise fool, the hero). Many of these appear
in popular films as well (such as *Star Wars* and *The Lord of the Rings*).
Children may recognize some of these characters easily, such as:

Cinderella character: rewarded for goodness and sacrifice

Superman character: uses powers to help others

Charlotte character: wise and self-sacrificing; gives up own life for
     friends

Robin Hood character: goes underground to fight evil and help the
     less fortunate

Summary

Teaching students to think between books, or other texts in the world such as movies, is an important part of teaching them to write well about their reading. Modeling specific ways to do this is crucial, because children do not know what teachers mean when they are asked to say or write something about a text. Giving children precise ways to do this scaffolds them for success and assures that they will be able to build conversations, and eventually writing, that are meaningful and deep about the many texts they read. It also builds an understanding of the interrelatedness of all literature, and it also gives a glimpse into the ways that humans have used literature to examine humanity and the problems that have always beset us. Teachers will want to hear students talking in these ways and to see some of these ideas in the notes and short responses they write, especially as the year moves into the third and fourth month of school, after which we'll be planning more formal writing about reading.

Teaching Literary Thinking Across Texts

◈ Model and specifically teach the kinds of connections you are making about the read-aloud; be sure to name the kinds of connections they are.

◈ Introduce the idea of landmark texts and refer to your own landmark texts often as you talk about books in whole-group instruction and individual conferences.

◈ Weave the idea of "That reminds me of . . ." into your conversation, as well as more sophisticated allusions for older children.

◈ Consider movies, TV shows, and video games as part of children's literary histories, as well as printed materials, and refer to these as you talk about books and model short written responses.

◈ For older children, use folktales and fairy tales to make them aware of some stock characters in stories; use these to think and talk about books.

◈ Using some of what you've introduced through talk, begin to write longer responses as models for children; as the conversations become richer, the writing should also.

Using a Readers Notebook and Making Plans for Longer Writing

When I taught fourth grade, I worried about holding my students accountable for what they read, particularly when I hadn't read the books. How could I know if they understood—or if they had even read—the books, if I didn't make them retell the story in writing? So I required my students to write "entries" in readers notebooks every night, long entries that retold the section they'd read, stated predictions for the next part, named characters, and recorded the number of pages and amount of time they'd read. Whew! What a tedious assignment! Today I worry that I made those students write needlessly when they could have been reading more.

The work of keeping a readers notebook should not be a chore. It should reflect a vibrant, vigorous reading and thinking life and a willingness to record that ongoing journey. The writing in a readers notebook should support thinking about books and should help scaffold students to write longer about those books. A readers notebook is a place to collect information and take notes, some of which may serve to record their thinking and reading of a text, and some of which may become the basis for longer pieces of writing. James Britton (1993) writes, "When we commit ourselves to paper the process of shaping experience is likely to be a sharper one than it is in talk" (248). So getting ideas down on paper will make them sharper, cleaner, crisper, both for the reader and for the teacher hoping to gain access to some of the reader's thoughts about text.

I strongly believe that students do not need to write long pieces about every text they read, nor do they need to write entries every night. But if teachers expect students to interact with texts, we surely can ask them to record some of their thinking and use it to assess their reading work, as well as teach them to look back at their notes to find connections or notice patterns to plan future writing. Looking at a readers notebook this way frees students to use their notebooks as workbenches for their thinking and to grow ideas and make plans for talk and longer writing pieces. This changes the focus of the notebook from "proving I've read this" to "recording my thinking about what I've read."

This defines the difference between a readers notebook and a reading journal, which is really what I asked my poor students to keep so long ago. A reading journal serves the purpose of proving to the teacher that the student has read the book by requiring students to write summaries or retellings after most or every reading session, to record the time spent and number of pages read, and to predict or ask questions. This journal exists to prove the act of reading to the teacher. However, the readers notebook differs in that it is for the reader's benefit, not for the teacher. If taught carefully, the notebook can show children that their thoughts while reading can have many forms, not just questioning or predicting, and that these thoughts are worth recording. The readers notebook sets children up to think about texts in ways that build strong reading muscles, while the traditional journal may become a tedious chore after every reading session, if not an elaborate lie about reading allegedly done. As always, we want children to know that reading is one part of their intellectual lives, and we want to scaffold that, not trivialize it.

If you have a writing workshop in your room (Calkins, 1994; Ray, 2001; Fletcher, 1996a), you may ask students to keep a writers notebook (Fletcher, 1996). This notebook is a place for them to record things that may become part of later writing pieces. To teach this, you may want to have your own writers notebook, because modeling for them is a powerful teaching tool. Using your own writing, you can scaffold the kinds of writing you want your students to do in their notebooks, remembering that a writers notebook is not a journal or diary but a record of ideas, observations, memories, and so on that may become larger writing pieces later. Some teachers prefer to have reading and writing in one notebook, because they feel the reading notes will end up as writing pieces later and therefore belong in a writers notebook. Others prefer to keep the two separate. You will decide what to do based on what you know about your students' ability to keep two notebooks and not lose them, or to keep reading and writing entries in separate sections of one notebook. I prefer two books because it is easier for me to assess reading and writing separately, but it is really a matter of choice. And the truth is that sometimes the boundaries between the two are fuzzy ("Does this go in my reading or writing notebook?"), so I think it's up to you.

As much as it may seem tiresome, keeping your own readers notebook is important for several reasons. First, it will give you samples of types of entries you may want your students to write; you can photocopy them or put them on transparencies for your lessons. It will also help you to be more reflective about your own reading, creating a vehicle for your own authentic responses. Most important, you will be able to deconstruct the process of keeping the notebook and anticipate problems students may have because you have had those same problems. When children see that their teacher keeps a notebook too, they are more inclined to see it is something worth doing rather than an assignment or activity.

Below I've listed some things we might teach children as ways to use their readers notebooks for tracking their thinking:

- collecting adhesive notes, writing longer notes, making useful charts

- using notes to write reflections, find insights, and grow new thinking

- rereading and using the notes as entry points for longer entries

- making plans for longer writing about reading

Collecting Adhesive Notes or Taking Notes

When we ask students to use tools, such as adhesive notes, to record their thinking, we must provide a way for all those notes to make sense. If students believe that adhesive notes are an end in themselves, they will quickly lose interest in them or use them unwisely. And frankly, we don't want children to think that writing on adhesives is "the thing to do." We want them to understand that writing on adhesive notes is one way writers can remember what they are thinking or record evidence as they are reading and that they need to take their thinking and/or the evidence and do something with it for the notes to be effective.

We also must acknowledge that adhesive notes just won't work for some students: Some children will lose them, or use them inappropriately, or just not be able to keep track of them. Those children will need to take all their notes in their readers notebooks, and you will need to teach them how notes should look: jottings in phrases, not sentences, no heading on the page except the book title, some indication of which page in the book the note is from, using abbreviations, using symbols such as arrows, drawing a line under notes to start a new category of notes, using T-charts effectively, and so on.

Sometimes students will just talk with others about notes they've written, but often it's appropriate to hold on to a note because it contains an idea, observation, or record of some evidence that has potential for more thinking (Figure 4–1). You'll want to teach children that their notes should contain small pearls of thinking that they might develop into larger projects. Adhesive notes like these should be filed away in the notebook, preferably taped in so they are not lost. Students can go back and look at these notes later, add reflections to them, or use them to make a connection with another text they are reading.

Once children have finished reading a book, they often wonder what to do with all the little adhesive notes they've put on the pages. Should they take them out of the book and throw them away, or should they leave them in as a gift to the next reader of the book? Should they staple them together into a little book, or tape them all on a sheet of paper? Clearly, not all adhesive notes are worth keeping, although if you teach students to use them wisely, more of them will contain worthwhile information. What children decide to do with them after they finish reading will depend to some extent on the next steps they take: reflection, longer writing, more conversation, and so on.

Sometimes teachers wonder how they can use all those little papers to inform their thinking. Of course, there will be less mess if you teach children

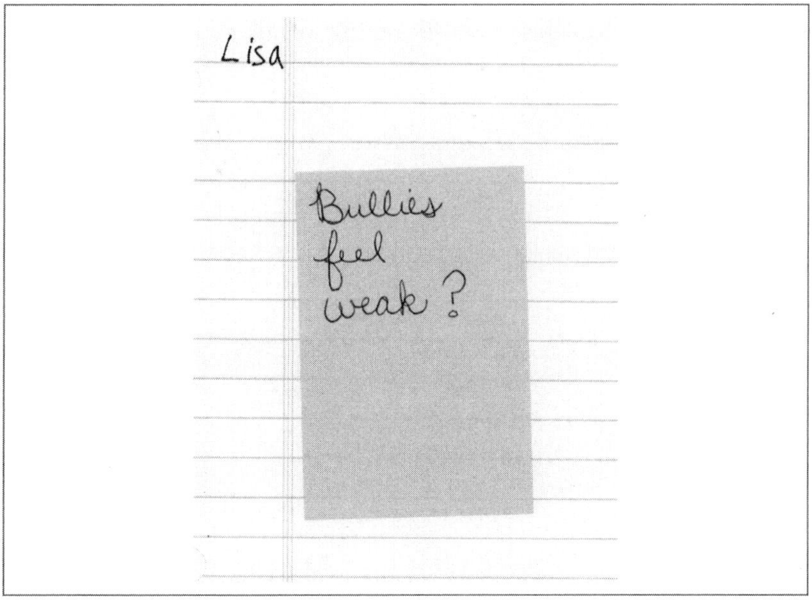

FIG. 4–1 *Adhesive note with potential for more thinking*

to use adhesive notes sparingly, and if you show them that the adhesives are small containers for their thinking. But you'll want children to know that once their thinking grows and they are "on to something," they can begin to write in their notebooks. Again, you must demonstrate how the notes could look and keep the writing easy to do: no headings, full sentences, or paragraphs yet (Figure 4–2).

I would suggest that one way for students to use their adhesive notes is to choose the five or six best ones from a book and tape them onto a page in their reading notebooks. They can read over and think about the notes to find connections, look to find a common thread in them, or just evaluate the quality of the notes they take. Rereading several adhesive notes thoughtfully and writing a reflection on the facing page can be a simple way to begin processing their note-taking. It can be an easy beginning-of-the-year way to evaluate student response, something to which students may return several times during the year. Asking children to hand in their notebooks with flagged pages showing selected notes with observations or reflections is one way of writing about reading and can be used for assessment in your classroom (Figure 4–3).

Students do not have to wait until they are finished reading a book to choose an adhesive note to keep safe in their notebooks. You can teach them to reread their notes at the end of every reading session in school or at home to look for any that seem insightful, and to tape those into their notebooks right away. In that way you'll be preparing them for using their notebooks even when they are still working on talking and taking notes.

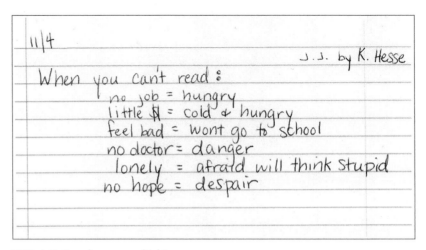

FIG. 4–2 *Sample notes as thinking grows*

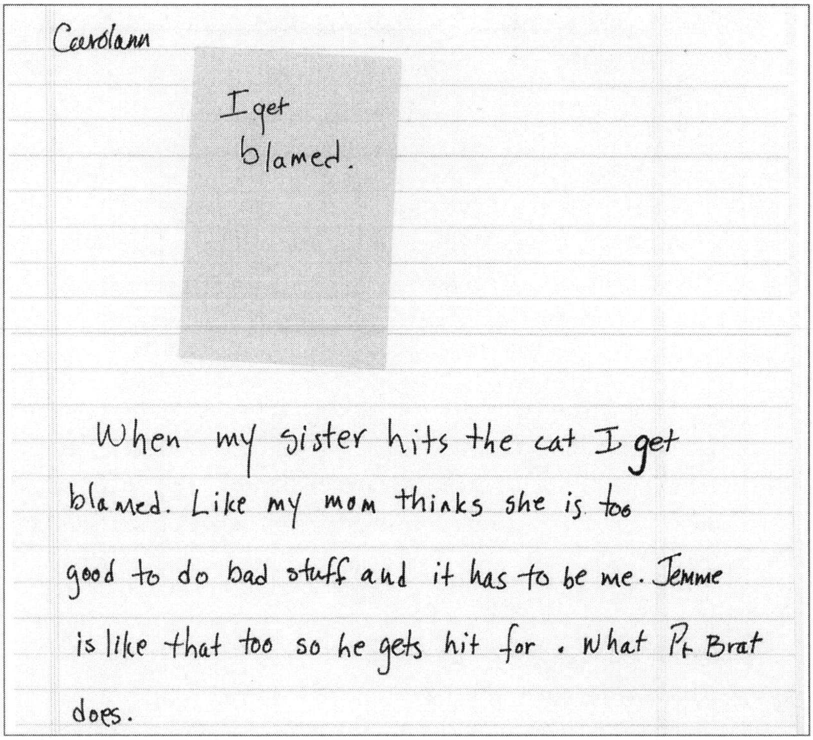
Caeolann

I get
blamed.

When my sister hits the cat I get blamed. Like my mom thinks she is too good to do bad stuff and it has to be me. Jemme is like that too so he gets hit for . What Pt Brat does.

FIG. 4–3 *Notebook reflections*

Another way students can use their adhesive notes is to look through them and find several that seem to trace an idea. Presumably, you will have begun teaching this sometime in the fall, so that students know that note-taking is not random, but that readers do it to gather information or to build a case for an idea they have. This is slightly more sophisticated than the first scenario, but again, we are scaffolding student thinking and teaching them many choices for demonstrating what they are thinking and learning. Students choose the five or six notes that best show the progress of their thinking about a theory they have, and then tape those to a notebook page. Once again, the accompanying reflection is the important piece, because that's where children demonstrate that they are synthesizing information and ideas.

You might want to vary the procedure outlined above or raise the bar as the year goes on by asking students to do this in other ways:

- Choose the adhesive notes that record evidence for your idea or theory about the book, then state your idea and a conclusion based on your evidence. Be sure the notes contain page number references. Add more information to each note by writing more about it next to it on the notebook page.

◈ Choose the one adhesive note that sums up your smartest thinking in this book and write longer about it in your reader's notebook.

◈ Choose adhesive notes that reveal an issue that you want to follow across books, such as how families affect their children. Tape these into a section of your notebook and add notes whenever you read another book that fits into your idea. Label each page of notes by book title so you can use them later for writing longer pieces across books.

If we examine student work, we can see that students can learn quickly to record their thinking and the confirming data on adhesives, preserve these notes in their readers notebooks, and then use the notes to expand their thinking to several sentences or a paragraph about the thinking they've done.

Rereading and Using Notes to Write Reflections, Find Insights, and Grow New Thinking

One of the most important habits students can learn is the habit of rereading their writing. This is essential for everything they write in writing workshop, but you also want to teach it in reading workshop. What good are all those notes if they don't use them for something? What good are all those notes if they don't synthesize them in some way to grow new understandings? Without rereading, much of what they write is forgotten or becomes something they do just to please the teacher. But when we show them how to lead literate lives, we show them how rich this rereading experience can be; so as their teachers, we must make time for them to reread their notes, as well as any longer writing, every day.

Often students believe that the notes they have taken are to prove they've read the book. Teachers do use notes to assess student reading—what would we think about the child who wrote on a note that *Shiloh* is about a cat? But if students are reading at the appropriate reading levels, then there should be less difficulty with comprehension. And if they are rereading their notes, they may develop a reflective stance about what they've written. Teachers surely want to model this for them.

Rereading in itself is just an exercise unless it has purpose and direction, so you'll want your students to reread while thinking of a few phrases, such as:

I don't remember writing that.

I wonder what I meant by that?

I don't think that's true.

That's a bigger piece of evidence than I thought.

Now I know how this piece fits the puzzle.

How could I have written that?

How does this fit in with what I know now about the book?

I've really changed my mind because . . .

Why did I choose to write that down?

How does this fit in with notes I've taken on other books?

What are trends or themes I'm noticing in my notes?

How do these notes help me plan for my reading or my conversations?

What longer writing pieces do I see hidden inside these notes?

The purpose of rereading is to get them thinking about the choices they make when they are taking notes and about looking for connections or recurring themes in their writing. One student noticed when she reread her notes that she tries to look for sibling rivalry in every book she reads, even when it's not a big part of the books. She realized that she was bringing her own biases to her reading simply by rereading her notes again and again. I would suggest stopping students from working three minutes or so before the end of your reading or writing workshop and asking them to reread whatever they have written.

You will also need to model the kinds of things to write on adhesive notes, just as you will need to model what to write in a readers notebook. You'll want to show them that plastering their books with notes is not as effective as writing just a few very smart, insightful notes. So you may want to teach them the following:

◈ Notes should contain only targeted evidence.

◈ Notes should name an idea or a theory about the book, not an obvious fact.

◈ Notes should be short and communicate something worth keeping.

◈ Notes are for them as readers to use for more thinking or to prepare for talking or writing.

Using Notes to Write Longer Entries

Sometimes student's notes, charts, jots, or webs will be all the writing they produce about a particular text. After reading some books, their notes are the writing they will hand in to the teacher. Occasionally, students will revisit their notes on a book later in the year and reread them with more experienced eyes. Perhaps you've taught a unit of study on story elements, and that helps them to see more elements in a text and to take better notes or to recraft old ones. It might even prompt a child to use old notes to write a longer piece about a book read several months earlier, to add more to the notes, or to look between the lines for more information. These revised or expanded notes, with new insights or perhaps connections to new books, might also be the only writing they do about a text.

However, some of their writing will be longer. In its longest, most formal structure, this writing will be in a genre of writing about reading, such as a book review or author profile, which will be discussed in Chapter Five. An intermediate step between short jottings with reflections in a readers notebook and literary essays is a longer entry about a text in the readers notebook.

These longer entries are written in the notebook and are quickly revised and edited to be graded. They should grow from the jottings on adhesive notes or notes on charts or webs, and they should demonstrate a student's continued musing on a text and a willingness to stretch some thinking. So by the middle of November, after students have spent time talking and jotting about books, you'll be asking them to take some of those jottings from their adhesive notes and expand them into longer entries.

Carol Ann, a fourth grader, chose three adhesive notes she had written about her book, *The Whipping Boy* by Sid Fleischman, and placed them at the top of a notebook page. She looked from one note to the next, rearranged them, and then freewrote from her notes. Expanding her ideas this way gave her some insights, and she was able to take these musings and craft them into a long entry in her reader's notebook (Figure 4–4). Later, she revised her entry and flagged it in her notebook for her teacher. Her teacher was so pleased with Carol Ann's work that she photocopied the notes and entry to use as a model for other children. With Carol Ann's help, her teacher was able to show the class exactly what she meant by "writing longer off your notes." You may want to use student work in this

Ways to Use a Readers Notebook

keep track of books read

draft and revise a theory about a book

record evidence or facts

note connections

muse on a text or idea

plan for longer writing

plan for future reading

plan for future conversations

build an idea

wonder about a text; record questions

collect interesting words or quotes from a text

play with genre and language

do some early drafting or targeted revisions (for example, trying several leads out)

dishonesty-
different
kinds

There are different kinds of dishonesty I think. Like there's the little kind where you lie that you don't have any HW todo, but there's the bad kind, like in the Lemony Shicket books. And in Roll of Thunder they lie.

Journey   - mother lies + won't come back

Baby - not telling something important

Number the Stars - not really her sister, but a good lie

FIG. 4–4 *Expanding notebook reflections*

way, with their permission of course, but until you can get excellent samples, you can write your own and use your own readers notebook entries.

These longer entries often reflect new thinking a student has done, as well as some risk-taking with the book. Without worrying about the constraints of writing within a genre, a student can preserve some of the spontaneity of talking and note-taking, and they can write longer entries about almost any aspect of the book, and in almost any way, as long as they show thoughtful consideration of the text. Remember that all this time you will be conferring with students, so you will already have a sense of whether a child understands the book.

Types of Longer Entries Students Have Written

◈ connections that helped the student understand the book

◈ comments on possible themes in the book

◈ discussion of why one part was important to the story or hard to understand

◈ questions about the book that remain unanswered

◈ what the book makes the student wonder about in the world

◈ how the student felt after reading this book and what in the book made her feel that way

◈ how the book helped the student as a reader; what he learned about reading and/or about himself as a reader from reading this book

It is also helpful to give children concrete suggestions for how to write more. By writing on a chart or overhead transparency, you can model the thinking you did as you expanded on one or more notes or charts. This gives children containers into which they can put their ideas. If you are keeping a readers notebook, you can use your entries as models here. Each item on the list below can be a teaching point in a lesson on what to write in a readers notebook.

What You Can Write in a Readers Notebook

◈ I can write more about a significant phrase from the book.

◈ I can connect the evidence together to support my theory.

◈ I can put my evidence in order from the most to least compelling.

- I can think about how story elements helped me understand the book.

- I can use what I know about story elements to say more about this book.

- I can reflect on how this book helps me understand people or the world.

Making Plans for Longer Writing

Before midyear, you'll want your students to be writing more and you will probably begin a unit of study on one genre of writing about reading. To prepare students for this, you will need to precede this with some teaching of basic strategies for planning longer writing. Charts, lists, webs, sketching, and short entries are all ways to get ready to write longer pieces.

Part of this work is to imagine what a particular note or piece of thinking could become in its next life as a longer piece of writing. Does it lean toward a book review or toward an author profile? Sometimes it will be a clear choice, for example, we've finished an author study and an author profile might work well, or some students will write to the author, others to the author's editor, and some to his reviewer in the *Horn Book*. Sometimes the genre will not be apparent, and students will need to try several genres before finding the right one. They'll ask, "Does what I want to say about this book work better as an essay or as a review?" And they'll try a little writing in each genre before deciding which genre they'll use. This work is best done in their readers notebooks. Some of these "try-its" may not become longer writing at this point, but later in the year students may come back to them and decide to expand them.

You will not be able to teach every genre in one year, nor would you want to. Some children may write in genres you have not studied formally and do not intend to study. This is the place for students to be independent in reading and writing. For example, I probably would not teach the whole class how to adapt a book to a play because I can get more mileage from writing instruction in other genres, but I would still encourage a student to try it as an independent project if she wanted. And even if her script isn't as good as I might want, it is still more beneficial for her to approximate writing in a genre than to make mobiles about her book.

Sometime in around the fourth month of school, students should begin to talk about what types of genre they want to write and make plans in their readers notebooks. If you search through magazines or online, you should be able to find some samples of several genres (book reviews, author profiles, and so on) that you can make available for the children to use as models. Let them read the samples and decide what they want to write and begin organizing their notes toward this kind of writing. After the holiday break, you'll formally study a writing about reading genre (see Chapter Five), but imagining longer entries can be very useful at this point. In their notebooks, students can rehearse for genre writing by writing entries that sound "book review-ish" or "literary essay-ish."

Setting students up for longer writing means helping them to understand that sometimes they'll extend their thinking about books and push themselves to write longer about an idea. You can begin by asking them to write longer about an idea in their notebooks or to choose one longer entry to revise and write out of their notebook. I would let them really explore an idea in writing, almost as if they were journeying with it, but I would make sure they were recalling some of the qualities of good writing I've taught in writing workshop: finding a focus and staying with it, using details purposefully, finding evidence in the text and quoting it, and writing in a logical progression. And, of course, I am always thinking about using punctuation thoughtfully to create meaning (Angelillo, 2002).

You can also show students that a readers notebook can be a place to stay with an idea for a long time. For example, if a child gets the idea from a book that elderly people are wise and often teach young people, he might follow and grow that idea for many months and across several books. He might also use the notebook as a place to plan for conversations about this or to give himself assignments related to it. And in the end, he may produce an essay about this idea and how it grew over several books or other texts.

Teaching children to flex these writing muscles in their readers notebooks will prepare them for the longer writing genre work they'll soon be doing and will give them practice stretching out their ideas before they are working with the constraints of genre. They can let themselves wander within the boundaries of the notebook and later go back to revisit some of that thinking to mine it for ideas for longer writing.

Summary

If writing about reading exists on a continuum from keeping adhesive notes in books to writing literary essays across several books, then children's writing must be scaffolded carefully. No one would expect a student pianist to go from simple exercises to Chopin polonaises, so we must not expect student writers to go from notes on adhesives to long writing pieces without careful scaffolding. We must build their stamina by providing opportunities for writing longer, on larger adhesive notes, on planning pages, and in their readers notebooks. Mobiles do not prepare them for this longer, deeper writing and neither do book reports. The work we need them to do is sophisticated and complex, so we must show and support them so they can get to where we want them to go in their writing. Keeping a readers notebook, going back to reread it often and thoughtfully, getting into the habit of writing reflectively, and even recording confusions can show children that a readers notebook is a powerful way for readers to nourish their reading and thinking lives.

Teaching Students to Keep a Readers Notebook

◈ Begin sharing your readers notebook with students early in the year.

◈ Introduce keeping their own notebooks after children have had some experience with taking notes on adhesive tags in their reading books and are ready to collect the notes in one place.

◈ Demonstrate choosing some adhesive notes to collect in the readers notebook and why (for example: "I think I have more to say"; "This is where I really began to understand the book"; "This is the strongest evidence for my theory"; "This is what I think the book is really about," and so on).

◈ Model writing more based on the notes; this can be more extensive note-taking, making a chart, writing a reflection, making a list of connections, and so on.

◈ Focus on the readers notebook by modeling several types of entries (recording, wondering, reflecting, asking, listing, webbing, and so on); offer these as a menu of possibilities, not as an assignment per day.

◈ Model using the notebook to plan longer writing by writing off a short entry, making outlines and graphic organizers for long entries.

◈ Demonstrate that some entries may lean toward a certain genre, such as a letter to an author or a book review.

◈ Demonstrate using the notebook to plan for future reading and future conversations, as well as social activities around writing.

◈ Establish a clear expectation for how you want the notebook kept and how often and how much children should write in it.

◈ Set up a clear expectation for how often you will collect the notebooks to read entries.

5

Genres of Writing About Reading

In the world beyond school, much of what we write—letters, journal
entries, notes to friends—is about some kind of reading we've done.
We send each other recipes with jottings about how we've modified
them. We send poems with notes to grieving friends or celebrating neigh-
bors. We write grocery lists for elderly relatives based on their doctor's
orders or make schedules for their medications after looking at the pre-
scription labels. We write notes to each other about books we've loved or
hated; we send emails to friends about editorials we've read in the morn-
ing paper; we write in journals about sacred texts or self-improvement
books we've read.

This writing is usually informal and for useful purposes: I need to know
to put less sugar in that apple pie recipe or Aunt Frances needs to know to
take two pills at breakfast. Perhaps I want to reflect in my journal about
my Sanskrit study or I send an article to my sister with a note about how
the information might help her business. This writing helps me to process
and use the reading that comes into my life every day, and it helps me to
communicate my thinking to others. It is one way we hope students will
make writing about reading part of their lives.

However, there are some people who actually write about reading formally and for publication. They write in real-world, actual "genres" of
writing about reading, the types of genres that are found in newspapers,
journals, and magazines. These people are writing in response to something they have read, and we can teach students to write about what they
read in the same ways these professional writers do. These genres of writing about reading are authentic, and we can borrow them to teach children to write formally about what they read. Children do not need to write
book "reports" or make dioramas or mobiles; they can write book reviews
and author profiles and letters to authors and editors. They can learn that

readers read these genres to help them shape their reading lives, to expand their thinking, and to connect with other readers in the real world. And they, as student readers and writers, can write in these genres to communicate to others their thoughts and musings about texts in authentic, real-world ways.

In this chapter, I will examine these genres, and look at how we might teach them to students in the writing workshop. I'll show how a study of book reviews might go, and how we might use this type of writing to extend the school community. I'll save a thorough look at literary essay for Chapter Six.

What These Genres Mean

Most people have read at least some of these genres at some time, but often we are fuzzy about exact definitions for each. The truth is that many of them overlap, and sometimes it is hard to say where a book review becomes a literary essay. Often we know one from the other only by the title or by the section of the journal in which it appears. The best way to get a sense of how each of these genres differs is to spend some time reading them.

You can collect samples of book reviews and literary essays from periodicals such as *The Riverbank Review* and make folders for each. Then look them over. What do the book reviews or author profiles have in common? What sets each apart from the others? What appear to be the identifying characteristics of each one? Once you have done that, the genres will become clearer, and you will be able to make decisions about which ones you want to include in your curriculum or which are appropriate for the age group you teach. In any case, you will want to teach one or two in depth as full-fledged writing genres and offer some of the others to the class as options for other ways to write about what they read.

Genres of Writing About Reading

book review

author profile

literary commentary

letter to editor, author, or other reader

interview with an author

book blurb or advertisement

literature in response to literature

play or scene based on a text

literary essay

Periodicals That Contain Genres of Writing About Reading

The Riverbank Review

The Horn Book

The New York Times Book Review

The Lion and the Unicorn

Voices from the Middle

Stone Soup

New Moon

Booklist

The New Advocate

The Ruminator Review

The New York Review of Books

Mentor Texts for Writing About Reading

After you have read several of these genres with your students in mind, you'll have a good idea of what each genre is like, but you'll notice that very few examples of these genres are written for children to read. Most of the writing is far above children's reading levels, and, given the need for mentor texts, this presents a problem. In the first year that you teach writing about reading, you probably will have to write at least one mentor text yourself for children to use as a model. So if you decide to study book reviews with your class, you'll have to study the features of book reviews, and then write at least one review that you think most of your students can read and study. I would recommend writing about a book you have read aloud to the class, so students can focus on the review features rather than the content of the book. In subsequent years, you will have student samples of book reviews, and you can ask children for permission to use their reviews from year to year to teach others. Most children are happy to let you use their writing as mentor texts for students in later years, but I would certainly respect a child's wishes if she were not agreeable to it.

Authentic Genres of Writing About Reading

Below I have included some of my ideas about each genre. Remember that often these genres overlap and that there is room for play within each one.

BOOK REVIEW Book reviews are written for the purpose of letting prospective readers know whether or not this is a book they'll want to put on their reading lists. Depending on the periodical in which they appear, book reviews can be quite erudite or formal. On the other hand, sometimes they have a chatty tone, almost as if the reviewer were giving friendly advice to the reader. There are short and long book reviews, and you may want to teach both types to your class. I will spell out a possible book review genre study later in this chapter.

AUTHOR PROFILE The purpose of this genre is to discuss an author's work in a larger context, rather than reviewing one book he or she has written. An author profile frequently contains some biographical information about the author, but only as it relates to the author's work. Generally, an author profile focuses on how and why this author writes. Since the evidence presented about the author spans several texts, it is a good genre for the end of an author study. Students might study patterns and features of the author's work, looking for these in the content, style, and genre. Examples of this might be: Gary Paulsen's wilderness experiences figure prominently in his writing; Patricia MacLachlan often writes about children whose mothers are dead or absent; Patricia Polacco writes about family and tradition. Weaving in events or facts from the author's life helps to lend credibility to the profiles, and making a point across several of a writer's texts is more appropriate than writing about only one text.

LITERARY COMMENTARY This is a piece written to examine an issue, using one book, series, or, more likely, several books to illustrate the reviewer's point. The main focus is the issue the writer wants to discuss, and the literature is used to support the stance or argument. The books themselves are not the focal point of the argument, but rather a larger idea the writer wants to consider. Some examples of commentaries might be an examination of how the Harry Potter books have changed children's fantasy books or whether listening to audiobooks can be considered reading them.

LETTER TO AN AUTHOR, REVIEWER, OR OTHER READER Letters should communicate some thinking, advice, or question about an author's books. For example, a child might write to J.K. Rowling suggesting a plot twist for her next book in the Harry Potter series. It is important to note that you would only write to a living author, since there is no authentic purpose for writing to a deceased one or to the characters in a book. And letters should be mailed, so children understand that letters can get a response. Readers may also write to other reviewers (in periodicals or in the class) or to other readers of a book. One child wrote a letter to a classmate warning that his review of a book was so damaging that it would keep others from reading a perfectly decent book; she would never have confronted the classmate face to face, but the letter was a safe forum. Class letters can be correspondences about a book between a current reader and one who has finished the book already. I would avoid asking children to write you letters about the books they are reading, because it may be mistaken for an assignment to check up on them and does not match the real-world reason for writing letters.

INTERVIEW WITH AN AUTHOR This is an edited version of a conversation with an author, often in question-and-answer format. Obviously, this is nearly impossible for children to do unless a willing author lives nearby or visits the class. Occasionally it might be possible to interview an author online. But children could interview other readers of a book and write what they responded, particularly if two or more students had very different reactions to the book. The interviewer needs to prepare a list of careful questions, get permission to tape the interviews, and work to cull, organize, and edit the information. Then they'll need to write an introduction and conclusion that show some thoughtful processing of what the other readers of the book said. Another way to do this might be to read several published interviews with an author, including those posted on various children's websites, then glean information from each one and write about them in one piece.

BLURB OR ADVERTISEMENT This short, succinct piece captures some characteristic of the book but leaves the prospective reader wanting more information, for which he will have to read the book. Students can write blurbs, or they can write advertisements in the forms of flyers, online bookseller ads, or the ads in literary magazines. You might collect these in a binder or display them in the classroom or school library.

LITERATURE IN RESPONSE TO LITERATURE Sometimes a piece of literature is so powerful that after reading it a reader is led to write something original in response. So a child might choose to write a poem after reading *What Jamie Saw* or an editorial based on *Number the Stars*. The original work should clearly point to the literature, and the student should be able to say why and how he wrote it.

In addition, you might want to consider teaching children to write the genres they are actually reading. Lucy Calkins (1994) believes that the best way to teach children to write about literature is to teach them to actually write literature; sometimes the mental work of writing a poem can go a long way toward teaching children what a poem is and toward an appreciation of poetry (Flynn and McPhillips, 1999).

ADAPTATION TO A PLAY Sometimes a scene from a book or, less frequently for children's writing, an entire book will lend itself to adaptation for the stage. If a student wishes to try this, I would make sure the text he chooses works well as a script and then give him the opportunity to stage the scene for the class.

LITERARY ESSAY The literary essay in elementary school is the predecessor of the writing about reading that students will be expected to do in secondary school. It is an examination of some theme or original thinking behind a book or it compares some element in one or more books. Literary essays often focus on a theme or on story elements such as characters and plot. Some examples might be: *Baby* is a book about silence and the healing power of words; silence is a manifestation of pain in *Flying Solo* and *Speak*. Although I certainly think children in the younger grades can be taught to think in ways that will prepare them to write literary essays, this is clearly a genre that you will emphasize as students approach middle school. I will examine literary essays in depth in Chapter Six.

It is important that children know they do not need to write about every book they read, but they do need to live their reading lives knowing that some books will naturally lead them to response. Some books will strongly suggest a need for writing, while others might be passed by in favor of some jottings. For those books that invite response, students will see something they want to write about. For example, they might begin to notice an idea, theme, or issue reappearing in several texts; or they'll fall in love with a genre, such as fantasy, and they'll read so many fantasies that they'll have lots to say about them; or they'll begin to see in characters' relationships mirrors of their own lives and experiences. If students are always reading this way, they will be filled with ideas for writing about what they read and will find the genres to meet those needs. Robert Probst (1987) tells us in *Response and Analysis* that the reason for reading is to allow ourselves to be changed by what we read, to open ourselves up to new ideas, to let differences rub against our beliefs to challenge, broaden, or even reinforce our understanding of the world. Remaining static as a thinker is unlikely for those who read. And identifying one's self as "one who reads" creates a constant curiosity about the world and interest in other people's stories and experiences (Smith, 1988). It may even be among a child's first steps from childish egocentrism toward increasing and gradual maturity and wisdom.

If we think of writing about reading on a continuum, then some reading experiences lend themselves to jottings or quick blurbs to advertise the books and others will lead to thoughtful essays about deeper issues. Some reading experiences are more memorable than others, and it is valuable for children to know that. In all texts, children must learn to read expecting to be changed by a text in some way, although we know that not all texts will do this.

Touchstone texts are texts that an entire class studies together when learning to write (Ray, 2001). Mentor texts are texts an individual student discovers and decides he wants to study. Although this is a minor difference, it does indicate to children that while the class has several texts it returns to again and again, students must also be looking out for texts they love and will study on their own. Thus, the class might have one touchstone book review from *Horn Book* from which the teacher will teach his minilessons, but each child may find her own mentor book review to study. Often the teacher will find a selection of mentor texts and offer them to the students. Some general principles for touchstone texts are:

❑ It is a text the class has heard read aloud many times.

❑ It is a text the class and the teacher love.

❑ It is at or slightly above the reading level of most of the students.

❑ It contains many things to learn about writing or about this genre.

A Unit of Study on Book Reviews in the Writing Workshop

Conducting Any Writing Unit of Study

Before you begin your unit of study, you'll want to think about some general principles for conducting any unit of study in a writing genre (Nia, 1999; Calkins, 1994; Ray, 2002; Portalupi and Fletcher, 2001). Initially, students need to have exposure to the genre through reading and talking about it. You could begin by reading aloud from that genre several weeks before you actually begin the study so children get the sound of the genre in their minds. Then you want to have children read lots of samples of the genre and sort through possibilities, deciding as a group which are the samples of the genre the class will use as mentor texts and which are not adequate or precise samples of the genre. At this point, you will still be reading aloud from the genre and steering the class toward choosing a touchstone text.

After there has been discussion of the features of the genre, children chart the ones they will try to put into their writing. Equipped with this information, the children are ready to begin choosing a topic for their own writing.

In general, the procedure for doing a unit of study is as follows:

1. The teacher reads aloud from the genre and makes many samples available to the students to read on their own.

2. Students study the samples together to identify and chart the features of the genre.

3. Students look through their notebooks for a topic of their own choice.

4. Students do preliminary work to organize their topic, gather more information or evidence, and discover any additional thinking they may have.

5. Students choose a mentor text.

6. Students write a draft on their topic using the mentor text as a guide.

7. Students revise to grow closer to their understanding of the genre.

8. Students edit and publish their work.

Writing Book Reviews

As I said earlier, the purpose of writing book reviews is to inform prospective readers; therefore, the reviewer is speaking as an authority on the text, not to prove that he read the text. This changes the stance with which someone writes and makes students understand the difference between writing to the teacher to prove they have read a text and writing some advice to a larger audience of prospective readers of a text.

In a book review unit of study, you'll choose whether to teach short or long book reviews, or preferably, repeat the study to scaffold children's writing from short reviews to longer reviews. I would suggest teaching both forms, as you want children to have a variety of ways to respond to a book, and sometimes a short review will do and other times a longer examination of the book will be necessary for students to say all they need to say. You'll want to collect several examples of the long and short forms and have each available on overhead transparencies for your minilesson. You will probably teach short reviews first and then back that study up with longer reviews, or you can teach short reviews in the fall and long reviews later in the year. Either way, you will want to have samples of both kinds of book reviews available. Remember that for now, you may need to write these yourself, as published samples may be too hard, or, in the case of some reviews you might find online, not written with the standard of quality you will expect from your students.

Genre is only one piece of the puzzle for creating good writing about reading. Student writing must contain all the qualities of good writing that you have taught in writing workshop. Writing workshop does not have a fence around it, and many children don't realize that all they know about writing well must apply to all their writing. Therefore, their book reviews must be just as organized, cohesive, and crafted as any memoir, story, or poem they write. Book reviews should also reflect what they've learned about nonnarrative writing through feature articles, editorals, and reports.

The focus of the book review study should be writing, because most of the reading and the mind work about the books has already been done through units in reading workshop, where students used adhesive notes and their reading notebooks to jot notes and save their ideas. They will use the writing process (Murray, 1999) to go from notebooks to projects—that is, they will use their notebooks to find ideas to write about, they'll draft,

Features of Nonnarrative Writing

clearly stated original idea somewhere in the first paragraph

information to support this idea that is grounded in a text

information organized in a logical progression to advance the idea

paragraphs that chunk information into categories, but transition from one to another to move the reader along

an ending that circles back to the beginning without restating it revise, edit, and publish—but the ideas they are looking for will be in their reading notebooks and on their adhesive notes, not necessarily in their writers notebooks.

An important feature of this, and any other genre study, is studying a sample of the genre to ascertain what its particular characteristics are. When students read several reviews or one carefully chosen review, depending on their grade, they generally notice some things that seem to be important in reviews. As students name these things, you can write them on a chart, or you may wish to make two charts from the outset, one for nonnegotiable parts of a book review and one for a menu of possible parts from which to choose (Figure 5–1).

- states title, author, number of pages, and whether there are illustrations (date published, publisher, price)

- names genre of book

- includes a summary or retelling depending on the length of the review

- refers to specifics in the text (could be story elements, events, outcome)

- gives the reviewer's opinions and cites examples from the book to support them

- states age and kind of reader the book is appropriate for

- has all of the qualities of good writing we'd expect in any other genre

- considers large ideas that the author seems to examine across several books

- makes comparisons to author's other books

- makes comparisons to other books of the same genre or to other authors

- draws connections to cornerstone literature

- uses quotations from the book to support ideas

- makes suggestions for improving the book

- refers to awards the author or book has won

- suggests the kinds of readers who might like or dislike the book and why

- states life questions to consider while reading this book, or themes in the book (Is it honorable to lie to save a life? Is any type of family better than no family?)

- comments on the writing or style (lively, lots of dialogue, too many characters)

- considers where the book fits in the reader's reading history (I am a different person after this book; I won't remember this book next week.)

- mentions if the book adds something new to a field of knowledge or a genre; mentions if there is an inaccuracy in the book

- states how the book fits in a series or how it contributes to literature in general

- gives constructive criticism

- names characters and gives some insights into them

- notes something unusual about the text

FIG. 5–1 *Parts of a Book Review: Students Choose from Possibilities*

Getting Started with Book Reviews

Remember that now students are working in writing workshop and that you are approaching this teaching as you would any genre unit of study in writing. This is what the beginning of the study might look like:

◈ Students study published book reviews to notice and name the features of this genre. The teacher writes these features on a chart.

◈ Students categorize the features to determine which are required in every review and which are negotiable or up to the reviewer's discretion.

◈ The teacher and the class compose a book review together (on a chart or overhead transparency) about a recent read-aloud book the class has shared.

◈ They name the parts they have included and determine what else they may have included or what else they want to add.

◈ Students look through their reading logs to decide individually which of the books they will write about.

◈ After deciding which book they will write about, students find notes, or responses they have written about that book in their readers notebooks.

◈ Students get a copy of the book to refer to while writing.

◈ Students talk with friends to flesh out their ideas and to plan out which parts of the book review they want to include.

Books on Writing You Might Want to Read

If you want to learn more about what writers say they do when writing, you might read some of the following books. They are about writing, not necessarily about teaching writing.

❑ Fletcher, Ralph. *What a Writer Needs*

❑ Goldberg, Natalie. *Wild Mind*

❑ Goldberg, Natalie. *Writing Down the Bones*

❑ Lamott, Annie. *Bird by Bird*

❑ Le Guin, Ursula. *Steering the Craft*

❑ Murray, Donald M. *A Writer Teaches Writing*

❑ Murray, Donald M. *Creating a Life in Essay, Story, and Poem*

❑ Provost, Gary. *Make Every Word Count*

❑ Ueland, Brenda. *If You Want to Write*

❑ Zinsser, William. *Inventing the Truth*

Books on Teaching Writing

These books take the processes that many writers use and translate them into teaching practice.

❑ Calkins, Lucy. *The Art of Teaching Writing*

❑ Flynn, Nick, and Shirley McPhillips. *A Note Slipped Under the Door: Teaching from Poems We Love*

❑ Murray, Donald M. *A Writer Teaches Writing*

❑ Ray, Katie Wood. *Wondrous Words*

Day by Day in a Book Review Study

Each day, as you plan to teach your minilessons, you'll want to be sure that you are teaching something that is significant, something students can generalize to their reading and writing lives and use over and over again. Minilessons are times for teaching by modeling and demonstrating, not by assigning work to children. So you clearly name your teaching point for every lesson and then decide how best to teach that point. I have written one possible scenario for a three-week unit of study in book reviews, but, of course, this is not the only way to do this study. Although I have provided you with a template, I encourage you to adapt it to the needs of your own students.

DAY 1 On this day, you want students to understand the purpose of a book review is to inform readers and help them decide whether to read this book. Readers read book reviews all the time; in fact, some readers develop sophisticated ways of using book reviews to decide on book selections or ways of interacting with the reviewers through letters. Reviewers include certain things in their reviews to give readers the information they need. Choose a book review (or write one) that closely matches what you expect your students to write. Put it on an overhead transparency; then show and name for the students some of the parts in the review, emphasizing that the reviewer has chosen to include certain things to inform the readers. Then provide book reviews on varying reading levels for students and let them go off in partnerships to study them. After the students have read the reviews and marked off the chunks, they reassemble to make a "parts chart" with the teacher.

DAY 2 Naming the different parts is one way to study how reviews go, but deciding which parts to include in a review must match the reviewer's purpose. For example, if I want to write that the plot of a book closely resembles another book, I may include a longer retelling to prove my point; otherwise, I may only include a summary. If a book has won a Newbery Award, I will mention that and perhaps comment on it, but I won't even bring it up if the book has not won any award. Some information can be tucked in, for example, "Newbery Award–winning author Richard Peck has a new book." (Because one quality of writing I want to teach children is tucking in interesting but not crucial information, I will show them how to do this.)

Today the class will compose a book review together. Ask students to decide on a recent read-aloud book that they'd like to review and to take a stance on that book. Based on that stance, the class will choose which parts they need to include in their review. Deciding which parts to include will depend on what the class wants to say about the book.

After agreeing on which part to include, students will go off in groups to compose the various sections of the review and then reassemble at the end of the class to put them together into a coherent piece.

DAY 3 To write a review, you have to have something compelling to say about a book and some strong feeling about it one way or another. Therefore, you must choose to write about a book that pushes you to say something. Students look through their reading logs or readers notebooks and choose the independent reading or partnership books they will review. They begin to take preliminary notes toward the review, especially recording the nonnegotiable items on the chart.

DAY 4 Before you can write a review, you must know the message that you want to communicate to prospective readers of your book. Students look over the books they plan to write about and decide what their stances or ideas are about their books. They consider what they want to say to prospective readers of the book, and they especially consider how to be original, clear, and fair. They begin to take notes on this and may need to study more mentor texts to see how to state things in a fair and honest way.

DAY 5 Reviews have a certain tone to them: some sound as if they are giving friendly advice, other sound more objective. Students decide the tone they want to use in their reviews and "adopt" some words from the mentor texts to help them do this. In their notebooks, they sketch out the chunks of the review, leaving spaces to fill in specifics from the book.

DAY 6 Writers plan before they write and sometimes use charts to help them. Students skim through their books looking for evidence to support ideas or stances they have taken. They may use an organization chart to help them sketch out the parts of their review, refine their thinking, and choose which examples from the book they will include and which they'll leave out.

DAY 7 When writers draft, they try to use words that will make their drafts sound like the genre they are writing. In book reviews, reviewers use literary words like *narrator*, *plot*, and *imagery*. Students will try to use some of those words as they draft. They will also look between the charts and plans they've made in their notebooks and their mentor texts to help them write the best draft they can.

DAY 8 Revision strategy 1. (*Note:* You must assess your students to know which revision strategies to teach, and none of my suggestions here may be appropriate.) Writers reread what they have written to make sure the content matches what they want to say. Today's work includes rereading for their intent (Did I say what I meant to say?), but also revising the actual content of the review (good examples, solid idea or stance, evidence from all parts of the book, clear opinion with support).

DAY 9 Revision strategy 2. Writers write between the parts of their piece so that each part flows smoothly to the next and each sentence flows smoothly to the next. Teach revising for transitions between the separate parts of the review. You may use mentor texts to show how to do this.

DAY 10 Revision strategy 3. The parts of the review need to support the stance you are taking. Students need to revise to include all the information they need to prove their point about this book. This might include work on parallelism, so that the parts seem to fit together and each hold their weight.

DAY 11 Revision strategy 4. Writers meet with others to talk about their drafts. Today the student reviewers meet with other readers of the same book to test out their reviews. They might ask each other: "Have I been fair to this book?" "Did I give too much or too little information?" "Are my examples strong and healthy?" "Would this review help you decide whether to read this book?"

DAY 12 Revision strategy 5. Unless there is a reason for changing, writers maintain the same tone throughout their writing. Reviews tend to have a certain tone (see Day 5), which students chose when drafting. Be sure your review has maintained the same tone throughout and that you have not changed your tone or opinion in midstream without signaling the change to your reader.

DAY 13 Readers must be able to read what you have written. Therefore, today's work is editing alone and with partners and using appropriate checklists that reflect what the class has learned so far about written language conventions and grammar. You may want to teach a unit of study on conventions (Angelillo, 2002) early in the year so your children will be adept at using conventions to convey meaning.

DAY 14 Students do some final proofreading to prepare draft for final editing by teacher; they meet with a partner to reflect on the process. Students consider what they've learned about book reviews and think about what other books they might review. They also consider how reviews might help them with book choice in the future, especially if the class begins to build a binder or database of reviews.

DAY 15 Students make plans for sending the review out into the world, reflecting on how they will make book review writing part of their independent reading and writing lives (that is, they are not done with book reviews, they've only just begun to write them).

Sample Minilesson

It is a good idea to follow a plan for your minilessons, which Lucy Calkins has called the "architecture" of a minilesson. This architecture helps you to plan lessons that are clear and cohesive, but any similar plan will do. The crucial thing is to remember that you must teach something—one clear thing—in every lesson, so that your students will walk away knowing something they didn't know before, and they should be able to clearly tell what that thing is. I have written a sample minilesson so you can see how these might go, but I recommend you study Calkins' book, *The Art of Teaching Reading* (2000), for more depth on minilessons.

Day One Minilesson

The purpose of this minilesson is to teach children that book reviews are written to inform potential readers about books and that they have certain features. Before you begin, you will have to find or write a book review that is appropriate for your class and put it on a transparency. Also assemble blank write-on transparencies, markers, and copies of several additional book reviews, which you will distribute to the class after the minilesson. As you will see, this minilesson prepares children for their inquiry into book reviews and shows them that book reviews are a type of writing that people do in the real world. Students are more apt to want to do writing when they know that writing exists outside of school and when the audience consists of someone other than the teacher.

CONNECTING TO THE ONGOING WORK OF THE CLASS Writers, you've been spending weeks and weeks talking and taking notes about the books you've read, and you have learned so much about how people talk and think about books. Now it's time to think about writing some of that thinking down and sending it out into the world to share it. One way people share their thoughts about books in the real world is by writing book reviews, and readers read those reviews to help them decide whether to read a book. For example, I read *The Horn Book* and *The Riverbank Review of Books for Young Readers* to decide which children's books I want to read next. You may notice some grown-ups in your life reading book reviews or even movie reviews to decide if a book is worth reading or a movie worth seeing. In fact, people write reviews to tell others about the books they've read or movies they've seen and to give others advice about whether to read the book or see the movie. So we are going to study how to write book reviews and today we'll begin a unit of study on that.

THE TEACHING PART One thing writers do is they study the kind of writing they are going to do to learn about it. So let's look at a book review together, and we'll name some of the things the reviewer included in his review. [Put transparency on overhead projector and read the review to the class.]

I noticed that this reviewer told us right away that this book was the newest book by a famous author. So that makes me think that one thing I might put in a book review is whether the author was well known or if this was a first book. [Underline that part of the review; then on write-on transparency, begin list of "features of a book review."] I also noticed that this reviewer tells us right away that this book is not as exciting as other books by this author. So on my list of features of a book review, I can write that a reviewer compares this book to other books by the same author. [Add that to the list.] So I'm beginning to get an idea of some of the things a reviewer might include in a review.

ACTIVE ENGAGEMENT What I would like you to do right now is to read this over and turn to your partner and say something else you notice the reviewer included in this review. [Listen to some of the children's conversations for two or three minutes.]

OFF YOU GO Let me tell you some of the things I heard. I heard some people say that the book review has the title of the book, the publisher's name, and the price. Yes, that's important. So let's put that on the list. I heard another partnership say that the reviewer told a little about the plot, but not enough to spoil the story for us if we decide to read the book. I'll add that to our list, too. So today I'm going to give you some copies of book reviews. I'd like you to read the one I give you and your partner, and then think about what features you notice in the book review. Talk about it with your partner, and write your ideas down in your writers notebook. Then we'll come together to share what we've found and to add your findings to our list of features. Any questions? Okay, off you go.

Sending Their Book Reviews into the School Community

Because the purpose of book reviews is to inform (or warn) others about a text, it is authentic to create ways for student book reviews to reach a larger audience. Having an audience for their writing raises the stakes for children; somehow if they think that teachers are the only ones reading their writing, it is not as important to them. But book reviews can be a wonderful way to make children see that their writing can make a difference to others.

Ways to Send Students' Book Reviews into the Larger Community of Readers

- Keep a class file of reviews as children write them, organized and cross-referenced by book, author, or genre; teach children how to use it and why they should use it.

- Insert student reviews inside the front covers of books in the classroom library or enter them on a class or schoolwide database.

- Teach students how readers use book reviews to help them choose books; ask them to cite which reviews helped them make choices.

- Accumulate different student reviews of the same book, especially opposing views; discuss the reviews with readers.

- Put student reviews on the Internet and check regularly for feedback.

- Include reviews from magazines in class file or binder.

- Build in time for students to respond to reviewers in writing or in conversation.

- Ask students to reflect on book choices they make as a result of reviews and describe to what extent the reviews influenced them.

- Teach students to reflect on which reviewers they feel they can "trust" for advice that fits their reading experience and on times when the review did not match their experience with the book.

- Start a book review club, where students write reviews of books they've read together.

- Include discussion of reviews of shared texts, such as read-aloud books.

- Make copies of reviews to trade with other classes or add to school library database.

- Make a class chart of quotes from reviews; make book jackets with quotes on them.

- Celebrate by making laminated bookmarks with quotations from students' book reviews and inserting them in the books.

When fourth-grade students at Village School in Syosset wrote book reviews, they entered them into the library's database. How exciting it was for them to know that their book reviews were available for anyone in the school to read. How supportive it was when students said or wrote to a reviewer that his review had made them choose a book or that the review was accurate and fair. How rewarding it was for student reviewers when other children asked the librarian to see the latest student reviews she had received or when they went to the database to read all the reviews before taking a book home (Figure 5–2).

Summary

Experiences like these let children know that writing for real reasons is not only satisfying, it's enjoyable and meaningful. Children who have written book reviews and whose reviews have become part of the larger school literacy community understand that readers write about books to communicate truths to others. It lifts writing about reading to a privilege and a responsibility for student readers. Whichever genres of writing about reading you choose to teach, let children see for themselves that this type of writing can make a difference to them as readers, making wise book choices, and as writers, seeing their writing influence their peers. Children do not

Grade 3
Harry's Back!

Harry Potter is back with his new adventure, *Harry Potter and the Chamber of Secrets*, by J. K. Rowling. It is Harry's second year at Hogwarts School of Wizardy, but Harry is warned. "If Harry Potter goes to school he will be in mortal danger, sir," said Dobby.

Despite this warning, Harry returns to Hogwarts. Harry Potter misses the train to Hogwarts with his friend Ron, so they take a car. But they don't make it safely because they get stuck in the whomping willow tree and narrowly escape with their lives. And the danger doesn't end there.

I really like this book because it has more action and characters than the others. This year the students have to go to dueling class and Harry and Malphoy are selected to duel against each other. In one chapter Hermoine gets samples from Crabbe and Goyle's hair and with that she puts them in a potion. She gives cups of that potion to Harry and Ron who instantly start to change.

If you love this book and you want more Harry Potter adventure, well you're in luck. Harry is back with his new book, *Harry Potter and the Prisoner of Azkaban*.

Grade 4
The Whipping Boy by Sid Fleischman

The Whipping Boy, by Sid Fleischman, is based on the idea that someone should take the blame and the beatings for the prince because he is too special to get beaten. The story, which won the Newbery Award is exciting and fun to read, but you have to be ready to enter the prince's imaginary kingdom in order to enjoy it. In the real world, no one should get hit for what someone else does.

Jemmy is a boy from the streets who is taken to the palace to be the whipping boy for Prince Brat. The problem is that the prince is so bad that Jemmy is beaten too much, even though he is happy he has food and shelter and he learns how to read and write. When they run away, they meet many rough and mean characters, and through all their adventures, they both begin to learn the meaning of friendship. But how can you stay friends with someone who is selfish and nasty?

The idea that someone should get spanked for someone else's bad things will make some readers angry. But it will make them think about how many times that really happens in families and in schools, when one kid gets in trouble for bad things someone else did. It also will make you think about what friendship really is. And the things that friends shouldn't do to each other.

This book will keep you reading and make you angry, but it will also give you a lot to think about. If you read it, you'll laugh and get mad, but you won't ever get bored.

Grade 5
New Pups Same Old Tricks

If your best friend has four legs instead of two then you will love *Puppy Trouble* by Marcia Thornton Jones. This story is about a small dog named Jack on his second day of school. But this is different from the 1st—there are new pups for Fred (owner of the dog school) to train. One of them, Buba, is a mini version of Sweetcakes who is a big bully! For example when Buba growled low and made Jack fall on his tail. How would you react? You will soon find out when you read *Puppy Trouble*.

And if you like this book then you could read *Top Dog* which is in the Barkly's school for dogs series. Not to mention that it is the newest book in the Barkly's school for dogs series.

I enjoyed reading this book because it had a lot of detail. Which kept me interested in the book. And if you have a hole in your tooth for dog books this would be the filling.

Grade 6
A Book that a Person Should Try
The Bad Beginning

If you are a twisted kind of person who somehow enjoys misfortune or sad types of books, you should try a book called *The Bad Beginning* by Lemony Snicket. This fiction book is the first in a series called *A Series of Unfortunate Events*.

The Bad Beginning might be different from the books that you usually read. This story, and the books in this series don't really have happy endings, which I think most books do. Also, throughout the entire story lot's of misfortunes happens to the 3 siblings who are the main characters. Don't get too nervous though, some not-so-bad things do happen—a few.

The 3 young Badelaire siblings are depending only on each other, after their parents died. Count Olaf, their new guardian and relative is plotting to steal the 3 siblings fortune that their parents have left them.

The Bad Beginning is appropriate for readers ten and up, because I think there are too many confusing big words in the story, (even though for young readers Lemony Snicket usually explains the hard words in the story).

The entire story is a very not-so-pleasant story to read about. But somehow it is an interesting read. Let me know what you think.

FIG. 5–2 *Student book reviews (includes teacher sample)*

Grade 7
Hoot is a Hoot!

You name it—this book has everything. Nasty bullies, tough girls, evil companies, silly adults, a new kid in school. All the ingredients for a great book, plus the idea that a bunch of kids can save a group of baby owls. Carl Hiassen, who used to write for adults, has written an amazing book that will make you laugh and cry and stay up nights reading. It also has the best book cover you'll ever see, with two little eyes that stare out at you and make you want to scoop up the book.

Rob is a new boy at Trace Middle School, and is having a hard time getting used to school, reminding us of so many other characters in books, like *The Tiger Rising* and *Tangerine*. On the same day he gets beaten up by the school bully, Rob sees a kid running through the town and decides to follow him. The mysterious boy turns out to be playing pranks at the site of a new construction for a pancake house. He has a good reason, because baby owls will die if they build the house, so he wants to stop them. Rob decides to join the fight, even though he wonders if there's anything kids can do to stop a big company. At the same time, he wonders if there's anything kids can do to stop bullies. Rob tries to do both things.

This book will win awards all over the place. Even if it doesn't, anyone who reads it will think it's award-winning anyway, because you just can't put it down. There is something in this book for everyone. It just has everything!

Grade 8
Just Juice

Karen Hesse, author of Newbery-award winner *Out of the Dust*, has written another book about families suffering in poverty. Like *Out of the Dust*, *Just Juice* shows the harsh realities of life with little money and little hope.

Juice is a girl who lives with her large and loving family. Like her father, Juice can't read and tries to hide it. She refuses to go to school, because it is too painful to face failure every day. Her father's illiteracy makes him unable to keep a job, and the family falls into hunger and debt. Juice's mother is too sick from diabetes to help them. When the mother goes into labor, Juice learns that knowing how to read can be a matter of life and death.

This book is less grim than *Out of the Dust*. Nevertheless, Hesse does not spare us details of poverty, hunger, and despair. Illiteracy is the dark secret that is the culprit for much of their suffering. Yet this close-knit family is happy, proving that while money is important to buy necessities, you can't buy joy. Readers will appreciate the happily-ever-after ending of this book, because this family has just suffered too much.

Teacher Sample Piece
A Tale of Survival

The Girl Who Owned a City by O. T. Nelson, is the story of Lisa and Todd Nelson, who are suddenly orphaned when a terrible virus sweeps the earth and kills all people above the age of twelve. Forced to learn how to survive in a world without adults, Lisa and Todd use their brains to think of ways to get food and protect themselves from child-gangs. When the leader of one of these gangs, Tom Logan, wants to steal everything that Lisa and Todd have worked hard for, the children must find a way to defend themselves.

I loved reading *The Girl Who Owned a City* because it was so suspenseful and shocking. The whole story is a puzzle that comes together piece by piece as each chapter unfolds with a tiny clue here or a plot twist there. In a world without adults, all the children in the story tried to find ways to get their world running again. Believe it or not, the children actually learn how to drive cars and build a city of their very own. And this is just the beginning of their accomplishments.

This story, which won the Newbery Award, made me think about how a kid, like Lisa, can change and overcome the challenges presented to her. I realized that anyone can think differently about herself. O. T. Nelson has also written another book about survival called *The Face in the Frame*. If you are the kind of person who likes suspenseful and science-fiction type books, then this book is for you.

FIG. 5–2 (*continued*)

have a vision for how writing about reading exists in the real world unless we show them. Teaching them to write book reviews, essays, author profiles, and other writing about reading genres will help them to see that this kind of writing can influence their reading, as well as their writing, lives.

Teaching Book Reviews or Any Other Writing About Reading Genre

1. Assemble samples of the kind of writing you will ask your students to write. Be sure it is on a level they can read, or you can write them yourself.

2. Include this genre as part of your read-aloud schedule several days before you begin your study.

3. Begin by having students study a text together, naming the features of the genre. Record these features on a chart.

4. Give students the opportunity to read many samples of the genre; also ask them to look for samples on their own, if possible.

5. Write a model piece for them using one of your read-aloud books.

6. Teach them to use their notes from their reading notebooks to inform their writing.

7. Teach them the language of the genre, for example, book reviews usually avoid the "I" voice, but still contain the reviewer's opinion.

8. Have them plan their writing and, draft, revise, and edit for publication.

9. Be sure to design a way that the writing will become part of the classroom or the school. If possible, send the writing to appropriate markets, including children's magazines, like *Stone Soup*, and online.

10. Celebrate! And plan for more writing about reading.

The Literary Essay

The literary essay. Nothing so defines a student's experience in English language arts as the requirement that he write literary essays about the numerous books in secondary English courses. Yet nothing stumps some students so much as the essay, this genre that requires they state their ideas about books in cogent, insightful ways. Literary essays hold such promise for teaching students to harness their thoughts on paper, yet so many children falter and fail. Why is this?

In the real world of letters, the literary essay is quite different from the school essay. The real-world essay arises from yearning to explore an issue or problem, to mentally knead an idea that lives in literature and in real life. An essay contains something that gnaws at the reader's heart until she must sit down and ruminate in writing, taking her reader on a "journey of thought." It is seeing the truth and the terrible beauty about life in literature and knowing that we read books because they show us who we are and who we want to be. How different is the school essay, where the student is required to fit his thinking into a rigid form, or to respond to an assigned topic, or once again, prove he has read the book.

I would not suggest that educators eliminate the literary essay from our language arts curriculum. On the contrary, I think it is a sophisticated way to write about literature, and we do well to expect it from secondary students. But I do believe we can do much to make essays more authentic, to teach students that the essay arises from having a compelling idea about literature that controls their writing. I also believe that we ask students to write too many essays, and we ask them to write about books in ways that communicate our mistrust of their comprehension, not ways that invite them to reveal and extend their thinking. If we establish strong reading and writing workshops, then students will be accustomed to having their own wonderful ideas and will have the investment in working over those ideas in talk and in writing. Essay writing is primarily a way to think, and as such, an essential part of what students need to know. If we teach children to write simple essays and each year scaffold those essays to become more sophisticated, then their secondary essays will be opportunities for rich thinking about wonderful literature. The students' ideas and their ability to think in a cohesive manner are what matter most in literary essays, not the ability to examine some idea from the teacher's head. And if we teach students to work over their ideas and write well about them, then on occasions when they must write from assigned topics, such as on state-mandated tests, it will not be difficult for them (Calkins, Montgomery, and Santman, 1998).

The literary essay must be taught well and taught early, but it is not a genre that fits into every book experience a student has. Some books cry out for book reviews, some for letters to the authors, and others for simple and thoughtful notes. Not every meal needs to be a dinner party; sometimes a simple bowl of fruit will do. If we hope to match some of the authenticity of the real-world genre, then let's encourage children to choose their own topics for their literary essays—topics that grow from having passions about texts—and let's be open to any justifiable interpretation. Let's also teach children how to write essays by modeling and writing with them, rather than giving them a topic and a formula and expecting them to plug in our thoughts. Let's give them concrete ways to stretch out and organize their thinking into chunks or categories, which will serve them well for the thinking work in every content area and for most of the writing they will be asked to do.

I'm suggesting a writing about reading gradient of difficulty, where students cut their literary writing eyeteeth on book reviews, author profiles, and the like. Then the experience of writing a literary essay can be reserved for advanced work, regardless of the grade. Literary essay should be taught as a genre of writing that fulfills a reader's purpose. Few of us are moved to write literary essays about every book we read, so why would we require that of students? It should be their choice. Nevertheless, there are some texts that we, as adults, might feel moved to examine in an essay, if we had a market for our essays and if we had the time and opportunity to write one. Students should be able to choose which of the books they've read leads them to write an essay. And if we require only two or three of these extended essays per year, how much more thoughtful and comprehensive will they be?

Some teachers may feel that students need to write many essays because they need the practice. I think they need the practice thinking and planning, and they need the practice writing coherent essays on a controlling idea in every area (see Chapter Seven). They need to practice this type of organized, thoughtful writing in social studies, science, and math as well. The essay is a way to write about any significant idea that takes hold on a reader, and students must know that these ideas can spring forth in other classes as well. Teach them how to do it—that is, find an idea, work it over, and plan it out—and then let them go to do it again and again across their days about any text they read.

In this chapter I will examine this most important genre and suggest ways we can teach literary essays to even the youngest students. We can scaffold their learning so that by high school they will be ready to do this type of writing in sophisticated ways. Literary essays are the epitome of writing about reading and we need to be sure students have all the tools they need to succeed. We'll examine:

◈ basic principles for teaching literary essays

◈ a unit of study in literary essays

◈ using literary essays to encourage global thinking

Basic Principles for Teaching Literary Essays

The first skill we want children to learn from an essay is getting a viable, meaty idea about a text, and the second is organizing information into chunks or categories. Sometimes a child has difficulty writing essays because the idea is not strong enough, and after a few sentences, she falls apart. Sometimes, the difficulty comes because the idea is really the teacher's idea, and the child doesn't have any notes on that idea or thinking toward it. In secondary schools (and on job applications and so on), students are asked to do this kind of writing about someone else's idea, but younger children need to learn first how to organize their notes from an idea, make those into categories, make the categories into paragraphs, and then write an opening and conclusion. Giving them a topic as a way to begin robs them of the chance to learn how to do this from the inside out. Remember that an essay is not just a formula, it is a way to think. If we focus only on the formula, students will never get a chance to work with the thinking part of it, and that's what they need to master first.

Because we want to teach the essay with an eye toward how students can take this knowledge with them throughout their school years and beyond, we can consider the important habits of mind we want students to learn. For example, each of the items that William Strunk and E. B. White teach us in *The Elements of Style* (1979) can be taught through the literary essay, such as making the paragraph the unit of composition, using definitively concrete language, and following the principle of parallel construction. Often we work from mistaken notions about writing when we teach children because that was how we were taught. So children are taught to use all manner of synonyms for the word *said*, when in reality, writers most often just use *said* because they want us to notice the dialogue, not the tag. Children are taught to go back and divide their work into paragraphs rather than being taught that paragraphs are units of composition and that writers think and plan in paragraphs. Children are often taught to vary their sentences randomly, when actually the writing principles of parallel construction make certain repetitions powerful. I suggest that going back and revisiting some of the books we read in freshman English can teach us so much about what we need to teach in elementary school writing and in what's important about teaching literary essays. We can look at one teacher's work to see how she worked on this with her class.

It was March, and Aliza Kushner's fourth graders had been writing all year about their reading. She had spent much of the fall teaching them to talk and take notes about their books, and in the winter, she had taught them some shorter writing genres, such as blurbs and letters. They had also done a unit of study on book reviews, and the students had enjoyed sending the reviews into the public. Aliza felt they were ready for a longer challenge, a genre that could really bring together their many skills. So she decided to teach a unit of study in literary essays.

Aliza knew that some children were thinking and talking deeply, but that others were not deepening their thinking as much. Still, she felt that the exercise of trying to put their ideas about texts into the container of an essay would help them, because it would teach them to think and write for a long time on one topic and to develop the stamina to do so. She also knew that they were well prepared for writing essays, because they had read lots of books as individuals, in partnerships and as read-alouds. They had lots of notes in their readers notebooks and a number of longer entries that contained ideas they had already begun to flesh out. They also studied and practiced talking about books from the list of "what to talk about in a book," and some of these conversations had become longer entries in their readers notebooks. They had studied several writing genres, as well as kept

> ### Some Books You Might Want to Peruse Before Teaching Essays
>
> Jacques Barzun. *Simple and Direct*, 4th ed.
>
> William Strunk, and E. B. White. *The Elements of Style*, 3rd ed.
>
> Joseph M. Williams. *Style: Ten Lessons in Clarity and Grace*.
>
> William Zinsser. *On Writing Well*, 5th ed.

Some Thoughts on Literary Essay

It is a journey of a reader's thinking about literature and how literature illuminates life and humanity.

It grows from having a hunch or idea about a text or about several books, a genre, an author, a theme, and so on.

It has the writer's voice, as well as the other qualities of good writing.

It takes the reader through the hypothesis (idea, hunch) in steps, unfolding thinking as it goes.

It acknowledges and refutes opposing views.

It is organized and clear, containing ordinate and subordinate ideas.

It circles back to the beginning without merely restating the thesis; it uses the arguments to come to a new understanding.

writers notebooks (Calkins and Harwayne, 1991), and they had gone through the writing process many times (Ray, 2001; Calkins, 1994). Now they were ready to expand those longer entries into essays. Aliza felt that with careful scaffolding, the students could write literary essays.

Aliza also wanted her students to know that essays can come from two places: What you think the author is saying about life through this text, or what you think about an idea and how this text supports your ideas. Each stance has its strengths and weaknesses. If you write about what an author is saying through a text, you are on shaky ground, because you can never be quite sure if the author really meant that at all. In some ways it is presumptuous to assume we can be inside an author's mind and know what she was thinking, yet clearly it is one way to examine texts. On the other hand, if you write about what you are thinking about the world and how this text or these texts support that, you've got to be thinking very hard and be fair to the integrity of the text.

The backbone of a literary essay is organization. Students must be able to organize their thoughts into chunks or categories, or put the information into pockets or "files," as Lucy Calkins calls them. Although it is essential to have an original idea about a text that breeds insights, writing well about that idea hinges on the ability to "chunk," or group, the information within it. This type of thinking spans all types of writing, whether it is organizing a feature article, editorial, or report into sections or paragraphs, a story into scenes, or a poem into stanzas. Learning to organize into chunks teaches children to discern the following:

- ordinate and subordinate information

- like and disparate information

- relevant and irrelevant information

- fact versus opinion

Aliza began teaching this type of organization in social studies. The class was studying early American colonization, and Aliza wanted them to realize that the great sea of facts they were accumulating fell into several clear categories. She used chart paper to name four categories that she thought students could recognize: the beliefs of the Native Americans, the attitudes of the Dutch colonists, facts about the land and climate, and the reasons the Dutch were colonizing New Amsterdam. As children collected their facts, they wrote them on adhesive notes or index cards and fastened them to the category on the appropriate chart paper. This physical act of categorizing information helped children see that writers don't plop down facts in a draft in whatever order they find them, but that writers are thoughtful and deliberate about where facts belong (see Chapter Seven).

When Aliza moved the students to literary essays, she did the same thing. She showed students that some information seems larger and more important, so that it becomes a category, and other information is grouped under it. She knew that sometimes students collect facts that don't fit into any category; some information is irrelevant or contradictory. Young students do not have practice with gathering facts and doing research and often find it difficult to assess information. They often are limited in ways they can find information and are not aware when facts seem unsubstantiated. Often what they do find is disjointed or irrelevant. Aliza decided to write a literary essay with them so she could show them what writers do when faced with each of these scenarios and show them that having found a fact doesn't mean it needs to be included. Writers are always thinking whether information fits their purpose, not about sticking everything in so they can squeeze out two pages of writing. Talking with students about their information can help give them a vision of what seems appropriate or what needs to be rearranged or left out.

> ## Steps for Helping Students Write Literary Essays
>
> Model, by thinking aloud, ways that we can think about books.
>
> Use talk strategies to get students to verbalize their ideas about books; emphasize the need to be engaged, to transact with the text (Rosenblatt 1995).
>
> Scaffold these ideas so they are "full," containing possibilities for exploration, and avoiding literal statements and prediction; set up "talk groups."
>
> Demonstrate jotting down ideas; teach students to take notes off their reading.
>
> Use numbering, Post-its, or index cards to organize evidence; consider ordinate and subordinate information.
>
> Lay out notes to look for patterns; consider which evidence supports theory.

A Unit of Study in Literary Essays

It would be unusual to do this unit of study early in the year, because so much of the groundwork for it happens in reading workshop in the fall. Students must be very adept at talking and taking notes for you to schedule this unit, though it certainly could happen earlier if your students have had several years of reading and writing workshop before coming to your room. Let's assume you are doing this unit in the late winter and that you hope to repeat it again in the spring or to ask students to write at least one additional essay as part of the independent writing work you require in the class. You probably will ask them to write the same type of essay about their reading in content areas, so they will have other opportunities to work in this genre.

Just as you did in the book review unit of study, you will need to collect samples of literary essays. Most are not written on children's levels, so you will have to write some yourself the first year. You can include some of my own and some student samples here. After that, you will have actual student samples to use as mentor texts for teaching. You'll also write one essay together with the class to give them an idea of exactly what you want them to do. Often teachers ask children to write something and the students have no vision of what that genre sounds or looks like. That's why walking through the process of writing a literary essay with them is essential.

In this unit of study, students will each write an essay about a recent read-aloud book. The teacher, who will write one also on a transparency or chart paper, will heavily scaffold the students' writing. After talking about her decision, the teacher will choose one idea from the read-aloud book for her modeling, and the students will choose from a menu of possible ideas for their essays. These ideas will come from notes of previous conversations they had on the read-aloud book, either provided by the teacher or located in their readers notebooks. Student will meet in "talk groups," so that the idea building and evidence sharing is a group effort, but each child will write her own essay using the information from her group. The teacher's essay will serve as a model, and the daily minilesson will walk students carefully through the planning, writing, and revising of their essays. In the end, students each will have produced an essay on one of four or five suggested topics from a read-aloud book. Then they will take the same process and produce an essay on a book of their own choice.

As we saw in the book review unit of study, the teacher's focus must be on teaching something new every day of the study. It is so easy to say, "Oh, today they'll just catch up on some writing," or "I'll just do some conferring today instead of a minilesson," but this is not accountable teaching. Every day we must teach students something new and something that they can use again and again, long after this unit of study is over, long after this school year is over. Teachers must be wise, then, when choosing what to teach in each lesson. Ultimately, you are the wisest person for deciding exactly what to teach your students, because you know them better than anyone, and you know their strengths and needs. So while I've given you a template for a unit of study, I strongly encourage you to modify or completely rewrite it to fit the needs of your class and to hold them to the highest possible standard. Ultimately you are the one who knows your writers best. You may want to slow down the study, but I would encourage you not to slow it down too much, as students tend to become tired of projects that take too long. Here is one possible way this study could go.

Day 1

TEACHING POINT A literary essay pulls together one or more significant ideas that a reader has about one book or across several books. Essay writers get their ideas from a need to express some important truth they've discovered in a book or several books.

MODELING Looking back at a read-aloud book, the teacher rereads some of his notes and makes a list of some striking ideas. These should be familiar to the class, as the ideas were discussed together when reading the book. The teacher models on chart paper or transparency how to list his ideas, and then how he plans to think and talk about them. He wants to decide which idea he will stretch into a literary essay.

ACTIVE ENGAGEMENT From the list of ideas on the chart, the students talk to partners about which one might interest them to stretch out. The teacher listens to what several partnerships have said and uses this information to shape three or four ideas from the same read-aloud book. The teacher calls the class together again and writes these ideas on a new chart, "ideas we want to stretch out." (Some students may offer other ideas that can be added to the chart as well, provided they are ideas that will yield thinking and writing.)

OFF YOU GO The teacher sends students off to join talk groups, each based on a separate topic. Students choose which group to join to have a discussion of one idea from the chart. Tell students to push their discussion of the idea as far as they can, so that by the end of the discussion they have come to a new understanding of the idea.

SHARE Students should look over their notes in their readers notebooks to find anything they have written on the topic they chose to stretch.

Day 2

TEACHING POINT Literary essays advance an idea and use literature to support the writer's stance.

MODELING The teacher thinks aloud about her idea and shows that as she thinks and talks, four or five chunks or categories of information become apparent to her. She writes each chunk on separate chart paper so she can add to them later.

ACTIVE ENGAGEMENT Students think about their group idea for a moment and imagine one possible category that might fit under their idea.

OFF YOU GO Students meet in their talk groups to decide on three to five categories or chunks of information under their topic. They write these on separate planning sheets or on separate pages in their writers notebooks.

SHARE Think about the chunks your group chose and be sure each one is equal in weight to the others.

Day 3

TEACHING POINT Writers find evidence to support their ideas. They go back to the text to do this and to their notes. They keep records of the evidence they find.

MODELING The teacher takes one category from the previous day's charts and, skimming through the text, lists evidence and page numbers for each category.

ACTIVE ENGAGEMENT Students look over their planning sheets or the planning pages in their notebooks and decide which category they will find evidence for first.

OFF YOU GO Using notes they may have taken in their readers notebooks, or skimming the actual text, students gather and write down evidence for at least one chunk of information.

SHARE The talk groups meet to exchange and discuss information. They assign themselves more investigation if there is a category that has few examples of evidence or appears weak.

Day 4

TEACHING POINT Writers reflect on their notes as ways to grow new thinking or to ascertain where evidence is missing or weak.

MODELING The teacher looks at each of the chunks on his chart and writes a reflection on the bottom of one of them. He considers how his thinking has changed, the strength of the evidence, and how it relates to the main topic idea he started with. He also decides where and if he needs to collect more evidence.

ACTIVE ENGAGEMENT Students turn and talk to a partner about one of their planning sheets and what they are thinking about that category and the evidence they are collecting.

OFF YOU GO Students write reflections about each of the categories they have on their planning sheets.

SHARE Students reread their reflections and then act on anything that requires action. For example, they get more information or they try to find ways that the reflections connect to each other.

Day 5

TEACHING POINT Writers use their reflections to help them have new insights about their ideas and to plan more investigation or conversation.

MODELING The teacher chooses one of her categories to examine; she talks and writes about how it fits into her main idea and how it relates to the other categories on her charts. She may decide she needs to gather more information because one category is weak, or she needs to talk to someone else about this category because she is unsure about how it fits in with her main idea.

ACTIVE ENGAGEMENT Students turn and talk to a partner about one of their categories and how it fits into their main idea.

OFF YOU GO Students reread each chunk they have written and think about how each fits in with the others and relates to the main idea.

SHARE Students will reread their chunks again to think about how they might want to put them in order.

Day 6

TEACHING POINT Writers eliminate information that doesn't carry its weight; they make sure each category is equal in weight to the others.

MODELING The teacher models rereading the categories he's written on charts, asking himself if each piece of information is worthwhile and relevant. He goes back and forth between his main idea and the chunks of information to do this. He deliberately will have written some information that needs to be taken out. He writes on a transparency that he takes out information that is weak, not connected strongly to the main idea, or that doesn't advance his stance. He talks about how he decides that something is worth keeping or needs eliminating, and that sometimes he is not sure and will mark it with a question mark.

ACTIVE ENGAGEMENT Students think about the main point of their essays and locate one category in their notebooks that they will read first in preparation for testing whether each fact belongs within the topic.

OFF YOU GO Students work alone and then meet in partnerships to decide which information to keep and which to eliminate. They lightly cross out information to be eliminated, because they might need that information again later.

SHARE Students think about where else in their writing they might be able to use information they eliminated.

Day 7

TEACHING POINT Writers organize their work before they write. One way to do this is to number the items inside the chunk and also to number the chunks in the order you will write them.

MODELING The teacher organizes the information inside each chunk and decides on an order for the chunks. She talks aloud about her rationale for choosing this order and marks her charts with numbers (or colored highlighters, or stars, or whatever). The rationale must include bringing the reader along from one sentence to the next so he understands the point the writer is trying to make.

ACTIVE ENGAGEMENT Students look at one of their categories and think about how they might arrange the information. They share this with a partner.

OFF YOU GO Students work alone to order the information in the categories and to decide on the order of the categories themselves. Students can cut up and rearrange the parts within each category and tape them together in the order they want.

SHARE Students share some of the thinking they did to decide on the order of the categories.

Day 8

TEACHING POINT Writers reread their notes and clarify exactly what they want to say about their idea. Then they write a beginning that tells the reader right away what their essay is about.

MODELING The teacher shows two pieces of literature where the writers have informed the readers immediately what the piece is about. (You can use the first lines of *Owl Moon* by Jane Yolen or *What You Know First* by Patricia MacLachlan, even though these books are not literary essays.) Then he clearly states the idea he wants to write about and composes a first line for his essay.

ACTIVE ENGAGEMENT Students turn to partners and say their idea in one sentence.

OFF YOU GO Students compose the first line of their drafts; then they continue to write their drafts.

SHARE Students complete the drafting of each category, except the conclusion, and work on transitions between categories.

Day 9

TEACHING POINT Writers write conclusions that not only circle back to the beginning, but that also show the reader a new insight the writer has gotten from the evidence in the chunks.

MODELING The teacher rereads her draft and shows how her thinking has produced a conclusion that grows from the evidence.

ACTIVE ENGAGEMENT Students talk with a partner about new thinking they have that grew from their evidence and that might belong in their conclusion.

OFF YOU GO During workshop, students will write conclusions that refer to their beginnings but that also draw new thinking from their evidence.

SHARE Students write another conclusion and decide which one is best in the context of their drafts.

Day 10

TEACHING POINT Writers revise their work. One way to revise is to make sure each sentence flows to the next, so the reader doesn't feel disconnected or doused with cold water.

MODELING The teacher revises his draft in one or two places where the sentences did not seem to flow into each other and the draft was choppy.

ACTIVE ENGAGEMENT Find a place in your draft where your sentences don't seem to work together and mark it.

OFF YOU GO Students work to make their sentences flow smoothly and find other places where they need to do so.

SHARE Students who used quotes from the book must introduce their quotes in some way. Quotes cannot stand alone without explanation.

Day 11

TEACHING POINT Writers revise by making sure they have written with the correct tone for their piece. In a literary essay, the writer is the authority on the idea and the book. Writers choose precise language to show this.

MODELING The teacher demonstrates certain words she wants to add into her essay because she wants her writing to be clearer. She eliminates tentative or weak language, and she lists on a transparency other phrases she might use as she continues to revise.

ACTIVE ENGAGEMENT Students talk about some words to look for that are weak words, such as *nice*, *good*, and *bad*.

OFF YOU GO Students revise their drafts to change weak language to strong language to show their authority on their idea.

SHARE Students share one place where they changed a word to make their writing stronger.

Day 12

TEACHING POINT Writers edit their work so readers can read it.

MODELING The teacher models rereading his essay slowly to be sure it has the punctuation it needs.

ACTIVE ENGAGEMENT Students edit one sentence while still in the meeting area.

SHARE Students who used quotes from books must use quotation marks and indicate the page number of the quote.

Day 13

TEACHING POINT Writers proofread before sending their writing to their editor. They mark their drafts in a different color so they can see where the changes must be made.

MODELING The teacher demonstrates using one or two proofreaders' marks in her draft.

ACTIVE ENGAGEMENT Students reread a notebook entry and use one proofreaders' mark in it.

OFF YOU GO Students proofread their drafts and give them to the teacher for a final edit.

SHARE Students think about the essay they wrote and prepare for reflection.

Day 14

TEACHING POINT Writers reflect on their writing and on themselves as writers.

MODELING The teacher reflects on his writing and what he thinks he might need to work on in the next writing piece.

ACTIVE ENGAGEMENT Students turn and talk with a partner about the experience of writing the literary essays and what they learned from it.

OFF YOU GO Students write a reflection in their writers notebooks about the experience of writing the essays, as well as what they learned and what they think they want to learn next.

SHARE Two students share what they want to become better at, such as organizing information or going from the planning sheet to the draft.

Day 15

TEACHING POINT Writers assign work to themselves as part of the writing life and as part of wanting to grow proficient at writing a genre.

MODELING The teacher shows her plans for writing another literary essay about a book that is not a class read-aloud. She uses her reflection from Day 14 to help her decide what she wants to focus on.

ACTIVE ENGAGEMENT Students look through their readers notebooks to decide which books they will write about next. They tell this to a partner.

OFF YOU GO Students begin to plan for the next literary essay, which will be an independent writing piece. They also plan for ways to make their current piece public, by putting them in a binder, on a database, or laminated cards in the classroom library.

SHARE Students share their plans for making their writing public and for writing their next essay.

Day 16

CELEBRATE! Students meet in small groups to celebrate the literary essay they just finished writing. After that, the teacher begins the next unit of study.

It seems wise to ask students to practice writing another essay at this point. They have just gone through a heavily scaffolded study, and now they can attempt to write another essay so they begin to take ownership of writing essays. Students can follow the entire procedure again as they write an essay about another book they read on their own or with a partnership or book club.

Using the Literary Essay to Promote Global Thinking

One reason for teaching literary essays is that children must learn to think about ideas and issues that appear in more than one text. Often many writers examine similar ideas, so children can find them in one text after another. Or one writer may return to the same issue again and again. After they have learned to look at ideas in one text, you can teach them to look for those same ideas in other books they may read or have already read.

At PS 59 in Manhattan, students write about reading all year. The principal, Leslie Zackman, and her teachers decided that children were ready to show their abilities in a culminating writing activity at the end of the year. They designed an "Across Books Study," in which every child in the school wrote about an idea that appears in more than one text. While the requirements for kindergarten were very different from fifth grade, the idea of looking for an idea in more than one book really took hold. Even the youngest students realized that ideas live in many books, because books are about who we are and how we live. Some students found they could think about books in terms of themes and that books they had read in previous years could fit; this created a way for students to talk to each other about books between classes and between grades and to consider how there are often grand themes that are examined again and again in children's books.

You might do something similar in your school if teachers were willing to plan vertically through the grades. Then the concept of looking at ideas in many different texts would be reinforced again and again. It also provides a cohesive way for students to grow their writing about texts throughout their elementary grades.

Grade	Number of Books	Final Product
Kindergarten	Two picture books	A poster with a picture of two books and a sentence about how they connect.
First grade	Three picture books or easy-read books	A booklet with a picture about a book on each page and a sentence on each page about how the books connect.
Second grade	Four short chapter books or nonfiction books	A booklet with two pages for each book, one page for a picture and the other for a summary of the book. At the end, write a paragraph about how they connect.
Third grade	Four books by the same author	An author profile focusing on an issue the author frequently writes about.
Fourth grade	Four books in the same genre	A book review comparing the four books and how they treat the same theme.
Fifth grade	Four books in any genre	A literary essay about a theme and how it is treated in the four books.

FIG. 6–1 *How teachers arranged the "Across Books Study," with modifications for the youngest grades*

Probably even more important than this is teaching children that books should change their lives. In their book, *For a Better World* (2001), Randy and Katherine Bomer tell us that schools are not separate from the world and that we must use reading as a place to teach social justice and social action. It is very powerful, then, to think about what literary essays could do for students in terms of changing the way they see and live in the world. If children are writing about social justice and thinking about social action, then the work they do in reading and writing workshop can have far-reaching consequences for them. Examining social issues through books and organizing their thinking to write clearly and convincingly can have far-reaching effects on education and our society as a whole.

Summary

Literary essays are not easy for children to write, but they provide a wonderful opportunity for teaching organized thinking and stretching an idea about texts. Although we would not expect the youngest children to write them, there are other ways young children can be scaffolded to think about ideas in books so that they will be ready to consider the concept of seeing an idea across texts when they reach third or fourth grade. Modeling provides the best way to scaffold their learning, because they

Grade 4
What People Have to Deal With in Order to Survive

Holes, by Louis Sachar, is about a common kid named Stanley who is found guilty for a crime he did not commit. His bad luck lands him in a very strange camp in a Texas desert called Camp Green Lake. As punishment, the boys must each dig a hole a day, five feet deep, five feet across, in the hard earth of the dried-up lake bed. The warden claims that this worthless work "builds character." Throughout the story almost every character has to deal with something in order to survive.

First of all, everyone at Camp Green Lake had to deal with digging holes. By doing this these kids are not getting their eight amendment right which states, "nor cruel and unusual punishment inflected." Digging a five foot by five foot hole in the stiff, dry, dehydrated dirt, in the hot blazing sun, is cruel and unusual. Also, everyone at Camp Green Lake had to deal with Stanley finding the pen cap with the initials K. B. on it. This is because the warden got excited and made everybody do double the work. As you can clearly see, mostly everyone at Camp Green Lake had to deal with many challenges including digging holes.

On top of all this, Stanley and Zero had to deal with a many things together. Stanley promised Zero reading and writing lessons in exchange for Zero digging part of Stanley's hole so that Stanley would have enough energy to teach. When the Warden finds this out, Zero gets very upset because she says that there are to be no more reading lessons from now on!

Another thing everyone had to deal with was the yellow spotted lizards. Everyone had to deal with the idea of getting bitten by one of them. This is because yellow spotted lizards need to protect themselves from the sun's powerful rays in the middle of the desert so they hide in the holes. And in Camp Green Lake there are a lot of holes. It also states in the text, "but you don't want to be bitten by a yellow spotted lizard, that's the worst thing that can happen to you. You will die a slow and painful death." Stanley and Zero had almost dies because of these yellow spotted lizards. This is because Stanley found something in the dirt and tried to dig it out. But instead, they found about a dozen yellow spotted lizards that started to crawl on them both. But since the sun was rising, they eventually got off.

Overall, in Louis Sacher's *Holes*, the characters needed to deal with a lot of different things including digging holes and dealing with yellow spotted lizards.

Grade 5
Teamwork in *Artemis Fowl*

Artemis Fowl by Eoin Colfer is an adventurous story of a twelve-year-old millionaire genius who tries to rob fairies of one ton of gold. Artemis' father was presumed dead which drove his mother crazy, so all she can do is take sleeping pills and stay in bed. The closest he had to a father is his servant, bodyguard and friend, Butler, who Artemis often teams up with. Artemis and Butler's trust in each other and their commitment to always stay a team is what makes their teamwork successful.

Bulter's trust in Artemis is a critical part of the success of their team. Without it, they could not work well together. Butler even tells him, "I trust you Artemis" Artemis then responds, "Yes. I know." Without that element of trust, the bomb the fairies drop on Fowl Manor probably would kill them both. Soon after Butler is asked, "But your sister. Are you willing to risk her life out of loyalty to a felon?" Butler simply answers "Artemis is no felon miss," showing that he will risk his and his sister's lives because of his trust in Artemis. This trust is what makes the teamwork between Artemis and Butler so successful.

Another element of Artemis and Butler's teamwork that makes it so rewarding is their commitment to each other and to stay a team until they die. One way this commitment is shown is when the author says, "Once a Fowl and a Butler were put together, they were paired for life." If they vow to always stay a team, then they must be very committed to each other. Another example of this attachment is when Butler tastes tranquilizer in the wine Artemis gives him before Fowl Manor is bombed. Butler could have tried to hurt Artemis since he thinks Artemis is trying to kill him, but Butler's commitment holds him back. Artemis and Butler's teamwork is successful because of their commitment to each other.

There are several examples of teamwork between Artemis and Butler in *Artemis Fowl*. One of these examples is when Artemis asks Butler to create a diversion so he can work on his plan to rob the fairies of gold. If Butler had not been there to create that diversion, it would have caused several delays. Another example of this teamwork is when Artemis needs to leave the security monitors. Artemis tells Butler, "We have a guest. I'll show him in. You get back here and police the surveillance cameras." If Butler were not there to do that, something might happen in another part of the house and the guest could be used as a distraction. Butler could also protect Artemis from anything the guest might try to do to him because if anything started to happen, Butler could run over to help. As you can see, there are several examples of teamwork between Artemis and Butler in *Artemis Fowl*.

In Eion Colfer's *Artemis Fowl*, Artemis and Butler's teamwork is what makes them so successful together. Their team is so successful because of their trust in each other. Another element that makes their team so successful is their commitment to always stay together as a team. This teamwork is shown in many ways throughout the book. In *Artemis Fowl*, Eion Colfer shows that a good team always wins.

FIG. 6–2 *Student Essays*

Grade 6
Special Things

Sometimes people have an object that has special meaning to them. In *Sun and Spoon* by Kevin Henkes, some objects have special meaning to the people in one family.

Spoon is a boy who got his name because his mother found an old spoon buried in her garden when she was pregnant. She thought the spoon was special because it was a baby spoon and had the name Fredrick on it. When her baby was born, she named him Fredrick, but nicknamed him Spoon (page 28). So the spoon was important to him and the mother.

Spoon's little sister Joanie collects sticks. Sticks are important to her. She calls her sticks "bones" and when she finds a knitting bag, she calls it her baby (page 53). Joanie becomes very attached to these objects and thinks they are real, which is not so different from thinking that something is "real" because it's been loved for a long time by a person, like in the story *The Velveteen Rabbit*.

When Spoon's grandmother died, he wanted something that was hers so he can remember her. He looked around his grandfather's garage and his house. He almost took one of her glass suns, because he knew she loved the sun. Finally he found her deck of sun-cards in the drawer and he took it, but he didn't tell his grandfather. Then he finds out his grandfather is sad because he wanted the deck of cards too and he thought they were lost. Spoon gives them back and gets a photograph instead.

Finally Spoon learns that his grandmother had an "M" on her hand for Martha, and that is best because everyone has an "M". He realizes that special things can belong to everyone, like the "M" on people's hands and the sun. He can think of her all the time, because the things she loved are always around him. Spoon learns that objects can only hold so much of a person's love. Sometimes we have to remember that it's what we have in our hearts that keeps them alive or that really matters.

Grade 7
What Kids Can't Do

Is it ever okay to break the law, even if it's for a good reason? That's the question Carl Hiassen makes us think about in *Hoot*. His main character, Rob, worries about that through the whole book, and some of the characters actually do break the law.

Mullet Fingers, the mysterious boy, breaks the law several times. He pulls out the stakes at the construction site, and puts snakes in their bathrooms. He lives in a truck, and he spray paints a policeman's car. He doesn't go to school, and he tells lies to the doctors in the emergency room about his name. He just doesn't obey the law, but he really wants to do the right things for the owls and for himself. Even though he has good reasons for doing what he does, he still is breaking the law.

Rob wonders a lot about what will happen to Mullet Fingers, and what will happen to the owls. He wonders how kids can change things and make them better, especially when kids can't vote or hire lawyers to help them. He wonders if it's ever okay to break a law. He feels very helpless, until the end when he figures out a way to do something without breaking the law.

If you think about history, lots of famous people got that way because they broke the law. Martin Luther King broke the law many times and even went to jail for what he believed was right. Other people, like Gandhi and the people who protested the Vietnam War, also went to jail for breaking the law because of what they believed was right. And sometimes people have to get the consequences when they do something like that, like going to jail or losing a job.

Hoot is not a book that tells us to go breaking laws, and you would never want to break laws for selfish reasons, like robbing someone. But it is a book that tells us that sometimes you have to figure out a way to make your opinion count. That's hard to do if you're a kid, because we feel helpless like Rob. Figure out how to do it legally, like saving the environment, because that's really the way to go. Just don't ever think you can't get something done or ever turn your head away from things you know are not right just because you are a kid.

FIG. 6–2 (*continued*)

can see the teacher's essay grow on the chart as they follow along and write their essays independently. Given the length and depth of this work, children would write essays about only a small number of books each year. It is a major project to produce an essay, requiring reading, talking, note-taking, and processing, even before drafting. With the exception of the one essay all children will write about the read-aloud book, children should be able to choose which other books call out to them for literary essays (Figure 6–2).

Teaching Literary Essays

1. Find (or write) literary essays that are appropriate for your students' reading levels.

2. Read essays aloud to them so they get used to the "sound" of an essay.

3. Choose an idea or theme from your read-aloud on which to base your own model essay.

4. Ask the class to identify several ideas or themes in the read-aloud.

5. Establish "talk groups" so students can talk about and share evidence about the theme they've chosen to follow.

6. Teach note-taking, categorizing, and eliminating or adding information.

7. Teach ordering information into large chunks and within each category.

8. Teach writing a paragraph from each category of information.

9. Model writing an opening paragraph that states the theme and an ending that contains some conclusion.

10. Demonstrate writing transitions from one category to the next.

11. Choose several revision strategies to teach (see unit of study plan for suggestions).

12. Revise, edit for written conventions, publish.

13. Be sure the essays become part of the larger school literary community or send submissions to children's magazines.

Writing About Reading in the Content Areas

The work of teaching children to read and write well goes beyond reading and writing about chapter books they read. Because deep and thoughtful reading and writing instruction is situated in interacting with a text, expanding and documenting thinking, and using texts to build theories, the same work can be applied to content area reading and writing. In fact, it makes little sense to teach thoughtful reading and writing only to abandon the same principles at other points in the day, such as during social studies and science instruction. Nor does it make sense to avoid nonfiction texts during reading and writing workshops. Donald Murray (1996) tells us that the same traits of good writing exist for nonfiction as for fiction or poetry, so we might think about ways to integrate the two and get more learning from each.

Many, many students, far more than we imagine, prefer to read nonfiction texts. They enjoy accumulating information about something that intrigues them, although they differ in their sophistication within these interests, sometimes depending on their age or previous knowledge. Some children get excited to find the most disgusting fact about snakes; others are outraged that humans are destroying the snake's habitat. Some students want to research Harriet Tubman's escape route; others become inspired to work for justice and equality. Some students become interested in the dangerous lack of sanitation for immigrants at the turn of the twentieth century; others see patterns of hardship and suffering for each new wave of immigrants. It seems that facts often get the strongest responses from children. If we get compelling, readable texts into their hands, there is a good chance they will read, think, and respond to them (Calkins, 2001; Harvey, 1998).

The implications for writing about this type of reading are vast. All the previous work on talking to shape ideas, taking notes, collecting evidence, categorizing information, drawing conclusions, and having insights fit into this content-based writing as well. Instead of making observations or thinking about a character or issue in a novel, they are making observations and thinking about a body of information on a topic of their interest. The challenge is to teach them to use the facts they uncover in ways that will help them think deeply, yet globally, about their world (Figure 7–1). Again, we hope to show them that they can use their information to write authentic genres, such as feature articles, reports, and news releases. In addition, we can teach them that other types of written text, such as charts, lists, and graphs, are authentic ways to organize and present information, as well as preparing to give workshops or have debates about information they've found.

If we look at ourselves, we see that much of what we read every day is nonfiction (Calkins, 2001). We read parts of the newspaper: headlines, the sports scores, editorials, movie listings, sale advertisements. We read recipes, the telephone bill, our child's report card, directions for the DVD player, a map, and dosage labels on aspirin bottles. We read pricing codes, washing instructions, invitations to weddings, grocery lists. And we also read book reviews, literary essays, and professional literature, all of which are nonfiction. We read these to get information we need or want or are just plain interested in finding. On the other hand, we rarely search for information from textbooks, so it makes good sense that most of the content-based reading students do should come from nonfiction trade books (Maxim, 1998). It would be unwise to exclude this type of reading and writing from classrooms.

I'm an expert and I want to teach you what I know.

I'm passionate about something and I want to tell you what I found out.

I'm fascinated by a topic and I want to pass on what I learned about it.

I have an opinion and I want to tell you about it.

I have an opinion and I want to convince you to agree with me.

I want to warn you about something.

I have some ideas and I want to explore them in writing.

I want you to go with me on a journey of thought.

FIG. 7–1 *Writing about nonfiction reading can come from many needs in a writer's life, but most important is the writer's desire to say or teach something*

We can look at authentic nonfiction reading and writing in several ways:

- ❧ reading and writing in a way that creates connections to the information

- ❧ judging facts as a reader and dividing information into chunks

- ❧ using information to create new thinking

- ❧ authentic genres for nonfiction writing

Reading and Writing in a Way That Creates Connections to Information

The ways you taught students to think and talk about texts in reading workshop (Figure 2–1) will serve them well in all content area reading. Some of the ways may need to be shaped to the content area, but few of them are inappropriate (Figure 7–1). They provide entry points for children to select topics or information within topics from the ocean of available facts. Donald Murray (1996) tells us that the same qualities of thinking and writing apply to nonfiction as to fiction and poetry. So thinking about what surprises me as I read nonfiction texts will help me to build conversation, take notes, and so on.

Part of what students need to know is how to decide what is relevant or not, so if I am searching for information on the lion's habitat, what I think about the Bronx Zoo does not fit in. It also helps children to understand that some types of texts are general, such as a textbook, while they can get more specific information from articles in magazines or trade books. Some of what children need to do is to grow common sense about their interactions with information and with texts. They must learn that although there are innumerable ways to access meaning in any text, not all of them are appropriate at any one time or in any one text. Like shopping in a catalogue, you only choose what you need, not everything offered.

Furthermore, it is unlikely that you will have taught every item on the list of ways to think about texts. The list is very long, and each item requires more than one minilesson. Some may even require entire units of study. For example, I can see that "larger observations about how this text illuminates life or the nature of good and evil" could easily be a unit of study off a compelling read-aloud or during book clubs in the spring. It might even be a way to incorporate thinking about some excellent nonfiction books into your read-aloud time. So although you might not have taught everything from the list of ways to access meaning, you undoubtedly will have taught some of them, and those can be points of entry into informational texts.

Ellin Keene and Susan Zimmerman (1997) write at length about teaching children to make connections to texts through looking at connections to self, to other texts, and to the world. This is very helpful for children, but you want to be sure they understand the intention of these connections. It is silly to make connections that do not help readers comprehend a text; so reading about trees and saying, "My Uncle Fred has a tree in his yard," without any thought for how that tree in Uncle Fred's yard helps me understand what trees do for the environment or how trees grow, or whatever, is useless. The connection to Uncle Fred's tree must somehow enhance my understanding of the texts. These types of literal connections may be a way to begin, but we must ask students to do much more than surface skimming. Keene and Zimmerman advise us to get the most out of connections by scaffolding student thinking and pushing beyond surface skimming to model deeper thinking. Connections must grow new understandings—so Uncle Fred's tree makes me think about why trees die, or how I have to take care of a tree, or why the leaves turn colors, or the effect the wind has on trees, or whatever. Listing some connections students might make can be helpful for them and show them which connections to keep and grow and which to discard as too feeble.

For example, Kahlil is a fifth grader who was reading a biography of Rosa Parks. He was having trouble understanding the book until his teacher told him to use some of the strategies he would use for fiction reading and ways to make some meaningful connections. They talked about which of the strategies he might use, and the teacher helped Kahlil see that two or three of them worked best for this text. When Kahlil set Parks' experience beside his own experiences on the school bus, he was outraged by the injustice Parks suffered and awed by her courage. He also thought of her study in terms of archetypal characters and plots: she was the quiet hero, like Frodo Baggins, who went on a quest for justice that had major implications for her people. Reading with a stance helped, too. Kahlil, who was not interested in sports, read many books from the standpoint of a boy who's been tormented simply because he's not athletic, like Parks was singled out because of who she was. Each of these things gave Kahlil a way to engage himself with the book even though the civil rights struggles of the 1960s seemed like ancient history to him. He went from text to self, to text to text, and text to the world. So one thing we can do as teachers is confer with children to help them see how thinking about texts works in much the same way whether you are reading fiction or nonfiction and to show them how to make connections that help them to understand.

Referring children back to the Ways to Think, Talk, and Write About Books list in Chapter 2 may help them as they read any informational text. One teacher asked her second graders to read at least three different science picture books on a topic of their choice. Before they began, she went over the ways she had taught them to think and talk about their chapter books and create connections that would help them access meaning. These were:

⬧ finding places where a text surprises me

⬧ ways this text reminds me of books or people I know

⬧ having hunches about what is really happening in a text

Having these frameworks in their minds helped her students think about their texts, whether they were reading about the ocean, spiders, or Native Americans. Children were surprised by the temperature at the bottom of the ocean rather than glossing over it as just another fact. Two boys reading about spiders talked about one of their read-alouds, *Charlotte's Web*, and how sad it was that their mothers always cleaned away the spider webs in their homes. And a small group reading about Native Americans had a hunch that if people let Native Americans have a bigger role in our society, there might be less environmental damage. Although the teacher modeled her own connections to text based on the three items on the list, she also conferred with children about what they could do, giving them careful support

gathering information (research in many ways)	eliminating irrelevant or inappropriate information
reflecting on the information	finding holes in the theory or noticing missing bits of information
growing a theory about the information	adding in information where needed
collecting evidence to support a theory	synthesizing facts and drawing conclusions
putting the evidence in some logical order	writing well using all the qualities of good writing
discerning important versus interesting information	choosing a nonfiction genre appropriate for the information and occasion
chunking information into categories	suggesting related areas or expanded topics for further inquiry

FIG. 7–2 *Writing skills children learn by writing about content area reading*

for their new thinking. The short list of "what to look for" helped give children a focus as they read, so that although the information was exciting to them, they were able to think more about it. Thinking more about information and creating some new thinking about it is essential for children responding to nonfiction texts, as well as to fiction and poetry (Figure 7–2).

Judging Facts as a Reader and Dividing Information into Chunks

One important skill students must learn is to organize information into categories. Students must learn to see that as they assemble facts on a topic, groups of information begin to emerge. Even if the topic is so familiar to them that they think there is no research to do, such as skateboards, we still must make them see that there are groups of information under the big topic of skateboards (and that there usually is something to research even if they know a topic well). So, for skateboards, it's not just how you ride them and that they are fun; it's also how they are made, their history, safety concerns, laws regarding use, proper clothing, and so on. Helping students group information or identify possible categories even before they start to research can prove invaluable to the thinking you want them to take away from this reading and writing. Remember that it is not that they learn everything about wolves or oceans or whatever, because they will forget much of that information (Smith, 1998), but that they learn certain habits of mind, such as categorizing information, which will serve them forever as thinkers, whatever the topic. Sparking an interest may be a by-product of nonfiction reading, but information changes so rapidly today and their interests will change as they grow, so ultimately it is the ways to think, research, and write that they will take away with them.

One Teacher's Unit of Study

Barbara Rossi teaches third grade at PS 59 in Manhattan. She wanted her students to develop the thinking muscles to categorize information in social studies and science and to write well about their content reading, so she designed a nonfiction writing unit of study. Barbara decided to do this before teaching the literary essay because she hoped that learning to put information into pockets would help students write paragraphs later on. It is smart to do this nonfiction writing before tackling literary essays because the same ways of thinking appear in both.

Barbara had already taught her students that their writers notebooks could be used for writing notes about interesting things they'd learned in social studies and science. She had shown them that the details of those content areas could be the parts of their daily lives that they might record for later thinking and writing. She had also taught them to live in ways that would allow them to be surprised and moved by the world and by the information around them. Thus, finding out about the ocean or wolves or electricity should spark them to think and write as much as daily events like baking bread with their grandmothers or riding their skateboards, and the things people did two hundred years ago should intrigue them as they considered their own lives.

Lucy Calkins has always said that the writer creates significance. Barbara wanted her students to read in the content areas in ways that would contribute to significance in their learning lives. She knew that learning facts doesn't change a person's life until they've done some reflection and processing of those facts, until they've created significance for themselves.

One thing Barbara emphasized was that it is never enough to collect facts. "Why would anyone be interested in reading a list of facts you've found about snakes, unless you told us something new about snakes as a result of them?" she told her class. "You've got to find the facts, that's true, but then you've got to do some thinking about them and figure out something new as a result." She used this as a way to teach children to set up categories of information, to establish a system for collecting information in each category, and then to reflect on each category.

Barbara decided to write her own piece about wolves. She collected three nonfiction picture books about wolves and read them, displaying them on the chalk shelf. On a transparency, she had written all the facts she had collected about wolves, and she showed the students how some chunks were already becoming apparent.

"When I look at these facts, I see that there is a lot of information on how wolves hunt, so I'm going to make that a category and write it at the top of another page," she said. "Then I'll highlight all the hunting information I've found in yellow. Later I'll go back and write all the yellow-highlighted facts under the heading that says, 'how wolves hunt.' I see lots of facts here about how wolves take care of their young. So I'll make that another category on a separate sheet of paper."

The next day, Barbara showed the class that she had six categories. Two of the categories seemed smaller, "what wolves look like" and "how they howl." Barbara showed the class that "what wolves look like" could be tucked inside other information by writing it as part of other sentences. So "wolves have heavy coats that are well suited to cold climates" can be tucked under the category of "how wolves hunt" because Barbara could write that wolves can hunt for a long time because their heavy coats keep them warm in cold climates. She later showed them that "how they howl" was information she decided to eliminate, although in the first paragraph of her essay, she wrote that a wolf howled, so she did tuck some part of it in.

This type of tucking is important if you want to teach children to write more sophisticated sentences and to use most of their information without all of it being treated equally. Teaching the idea of recognizing ordinate and subordinate facts is crucial, because often children treat all facts equally. Some facts are just not as important as others, or come under larger headings, or don't really belong anywhere, but are interesting. So children must learn that they have to judge facts: what is important versus what is interesting. We must know how wolves hunt, because otherwise we won't understand wolves, but we don't need to understand how they howl, unless this is a report on how animals communicate. That's the difference between important and interesting facts. Children may not need to eliminate facts that are interesting but not important; they just have to figure out how to tuck them in smoothly.

Barbara made a T-chart of her facts about wolves and labeled it "interesting" and "important." She showed children that sometimes she moved a fact from one side of the chart to the other as she carefully considered it. Sometimes she reluctantly crossed off an interesting fact because she had no place to use it, but sometimes she was able to tuck that fact inside other facts. When she was able to do this, she said she celebrated, because she got to use something interesting without confusing her reader, or getting off course, or sounding choppy.

Probably the most important thing to teach in informational writing is that it is not enough to collect a bunch of interesting facts and stick them all in your writing. The most important thing is that you have to do some thinking about those facts and come up with something new to say. This is not easy for children; most of them think it's just fine if they can hand a few facts to the teacher. But that is not enough. Because we want children to be changed by what they read, and to use some of that change as the basis for their writing, they also need to be changed by the facts they collect on a topic.

Barbara demonstrated this to her class by rereading her list of facts from the overhead transparency. She modeled forcing herself to think and talk about the facts, not letting them remain static on the page. As she reread her facts, she told the class that they made her think that wolves are very

One Student's Nonfiction Writing

One student, Carmela, wanted to write about Yorkshire terriers. Earlier in the year, she had written a memoir about the day she brought her puppy home on the subway hidden inside her coat. Now she wanted to write a feature article about Yorkies. Carmela had lots of facts about them from several reference books she had brought from home. She was passionate about her topic and had done her research, writing each fact on a separate index card. Carmela was writing as an expert, not as a third grader writing to prove she'd read some books. In fact, the other students were looking forward to reading what she wrote, because they knew Carmela had smart things to say about Yorkies. After reflecting on her information, Carmela realized that what she wanted to tell people was that Yorkshire terriers are perfect dogs for apartment dwellers. So she combed through all the facts and highlighted the ones that supported her idea—they are small, they don't need lots of exercise, they are good watchdogs. After that, it was easy for her to organize her writing because she knew exactly what she wanted to say and why she wanted to say it.

much like humans; after all, they go out to get food every day, they live in families, they protect their babies. So next to each chunk of facts, she wrote a reflection on how that chunk fit in with her idea about wolves. Once again, Barbara was showing her students that you have to have an idea about your reading—you can't just let facts parade in front of your eyes without responding to them in some way. Reflecting on what they might mean or how they go together is one way to make sense of them.

Barbara looked over her facts about wolves and decided that there were some facts that didn't fit with her idea. They didn't disprove her idea, but they didn't support it either. So she showed her class how she removed irrelevant facts from her list. "I won't cross them off for good," she said. "I know that they are good facts, so I might use them in another writing piece. I'll save them by putting a box around them and marking them with a blue X. That tells me not to use them in this piece, but to hold on to them." Barbara knew some children had written their facts on index cards, so for them it was easier to put the cards into piles or chunks and to remove some from the bunch to save for later. Other students had taken their notes on loose-leaf paper, so they needed to cut up the pages to arrange the facts into chunks and to order the information within the chunks. Information that did not fit with their idea and reflection was taped into their notebooks to save for another time. It was good information; it just did not fit with their idea.

Barbara was ready to write her essay on an overhead transparency. She talked through her ideas for how she would arrange the information chunks, starting with the least compelling chunk to the most compelling one. She wanted her readers to get the sense that her evidence to support her argument got stronger as they continued to read. She decided to order her information carefully: first, that wolves are devoted parents and care for their babies; second, that they live in extended families under one roof, and third, that some go out every day to find food, just as humans go to work to make money for necessities or to buy food. Each fact she chose supported her contention that wolves are more like humans than humans would care to admit.

All this modeling allowed students to follow their teacher's thinking and writing carefully. Barbara made sure students were keeping with her by frequently conferring with them (Anderson, 2000) and by looking over their notes regularly. She was less interested in the viability of their ideas at this point than she was in their ability to generate an idea from a group of facts and prove it. Although their end products sounded very similar to Barbara's writing, she was convinced that they had learned some valuable skills about writing about nonfiction reading.

Using Information to Create New Thinking

Because finding information is not a goal in itself, we want children to be able to think about the facts they find.

Kerry Moscato wanted her sixth graders to do the same thing that Barbara wanted her third graders to do, but Kerry wanted it to fold into work she was doing with author profiles. She had noticed that her students were adept at collecting information about authors and reporting it back in a sequential way, but she felt they needed to push their thinking further. "What good are facts if you don't use them to think?" she told her class. "If I wanted the facts, I could go read the same books you did or go to the same websites."

So Kerry designed a sheet that students would use to show their thinking as they collected facts. She wanted them to reflect on each new bit of information, rather than just collect, collect, collect. For each new fact, they had to slow down and reflect.

She asked them:

◈ What other information does this new fact support?

◈ How does this new fact add to my store of knowledge or push it in a new direction?

◈ How does it fit in with what I already know?

◈ What am I thinking now that I know this?

Kerry was most interested in nurturing their ability to use facts to think. The reflection piece of their writing sheet mattered to her as much as the facts and citations themselves. In the end, her students used this reflection to make observations about nonfiction topics that proved they were using information to grow ideas.

Authentic Genres for Nonfiction Writing

Just as we thought about the authentic ways students can write about books in general, we can see that they can write in the same ways about nonfiction. So students could write a book review of a new book on Dr. Martin Luther King or an author profile of Seymour Simon, who writes many nonfiction trade books for children. On the other hand, there are some genres that are uniquely suited to the reading of nonfiction, and you might decide to teach those as part of your writing workshop, while students are reading the information in reading workshop, or during content area study.

Three genres come to mind as good possibilities for children to write, although there are many more as we consider real-world genres of writing about reading. The three I'll examine here are reports, feature articles, and editorials, but you could certainly teach others, including news articles, charts and lists for presentations, and op-ed pieces. Within the ones I have chosen, there is a host of smaller writing genres to teach, including writing captions for charts or pictures and writing interesting subheadings. You can get a lot of teaching through these three genres, but I would encourage you to try others if you want.

I like to think of these genres as being on a continuum from most factual to most opinion-based. In a report, students are presenting facts they've uncovered through experience and/or research. And although no one would go to an eight-year-old for the definitive word on snakes, the report is a real-world genre that people write in every day. (In fact, few of us would go to an eight-year-old for the definitive word on most things, so for our purposes here, let's agree to accept their childish versions of any genre.) If we want children to write reports, then let's make it the smartest writing with the most carry-through teaching we can. To do this, we'll need to focus on the writing rather than the topic itself.

For younger children or those who are less experienced, it might be helpful to set up a progression of how you will teach these genres. For example, you might want to teach report writing first, as it is clear and leans on factual information, and the work children need to do first involves organizing and clearly presenting facts. But after they have lived with their facts for a long time, children are ready to write feature articles. The articles differ in the sense that writers first must organize the facts they have collected, but then decide which ones (and in what sequence) to include to support an angle on the information. Finally, children might be ready to write an editorial based on the facts, because by this time they have internalized them and have grown some thinking about how these facts change who they are or what they think about the world. If you are doing these back-to-back, children use the same topic to go from one genre to the next, growing more and more opinion based on the facts. They can use the same facts but flip the writing into another genre by manipulating which facts to include, and what order to include them in, to support an angle in the feature article or a strong opinion in the editorial.

It is also good for students to learn that writers often reuse their information. If a writer does a great deal of research on, say, the Civil War, he will want to use that information again and again. He might write a book about most of it, some articles about different aspects of it, a letter to a congressman about some of it, give a presentation on it, and write an editorial based on opinions he has formed from knowing it so well. When you live with a collection of facts for a while, you can't help but do some reflection on them. Writers even angle their information differently depending on their audience or the magazine for which they are writing, so the same information on the Civil War will sound different if I'm writing for *Civil War Times* than if I'm writing for *Cobblestone*. The child who writes about skateboard will write differently if he's writing for his peers, who presumably know a lot about skateboards and are experts, than he would write for *Time* magazine or *My Generation* (formerly *Modern Maturity*). And yes, I know it's unlikely he'd write for them, but you get the point. It helps for children to think of possible markets, because it helps them to understand that teachers are not their only audience.

Similarly, he would write the article differently depending on his slant or angle. If his slant or angle is that skateboards are great and you should give them a try, he'd include different facts than if his angle is that skateboards are dangerous and you need to take some precautions. For an editorial, he might establish a strong opinion, as strong as "everyone should use skateboards instead of cars to save the environment" or that "they should be banned because they're a public menace." And the facts he includes will depend on his stance.

Using well-researched facts to write editorials lifts this genre above the typical things kids write about, such as how the food in the cafeteria is awful and whether kids should wear uniforms. I do not mean to trivialize their ideas or opinions, but I want us to demonstrate to them that having an opinion comes from knowing a lot about something and from doing the research to support it. Certainly I have seen some decent student editorials on school uniforms, but those were based on previous research that students had done on the clothing and the effect of wearing uniforms in general, not on just an opinion. And I do believe that children can write

Use these ways to think about the facts you've collected. You might choose to make a double-paged entry in your notebook or a T-chart.

- looking across facts to discern categories of information

- looking between facts for commonalities

- finding ways these facts fit in with other things you know

- finding places where information seems to be missing

- thinking about facts throughout the day to find more connections

- talking with others about the facts and recording what that makes you think

- "talking back to" or questioning the facts to develop a stance: for example, thinking, How could that be? That seems like it's so much or too big! I can't believe it! This can't be true! What on earth does that mean? I never knew that!

FIG. 7–3 *Reflecting on facts in a readers notebook*

excellent reports about skateboards, rap music, and television programming, provided they research and read about these topics and have more to say than, "This is cool." Again, focusing on the need for facts to give birth to ideas will help you teach children to write powerful and persuasive editorials (Figure 7–3).

On the other hand, you might choose to teach only one unit of study in this type of writing, but if you do that, I strongly urge you to choose the feature article. In terms of writing about reading, teaching only report writing will not make it clear to students that it's not enough to tell us some information, they have to think something new about it and tell us that, too. And teaching only the editorial will not give them enough rehearsal time in reading and processing some facts.

Below I've included a possible plan for a unit of study on report writing, with ways you could modify it for older children or for feature articles and/or editorials. I realize that some teachers will find this degree of detail on how to teach a unit unnecessary, but I offer it as a template. Should you choose to use it, feel free to modify it based on what you know about your students as readers and writers and based on the grade level you teach.

A Unit of Study in Writing About Nonfiction Reading

Before you begin the study, you will need to find several published texts that are like the kind of text you want your students to write. In subsequent years, you might use fine student writing that you'll get from the first time you do the study, but for now you'll need to look for texts that are reports, feature articles, or editorials. Begin reading aloud from the genre before you begin the study, so children learn to hear what the genre sounds like.

You'll also need to determine whether you want students to write about a current inquiry you are doing in science or social studies or whether you will open it up to any interest they might have. I recommend narrowing it at first to content area topics, mainly because it will be easier for you to provide selected trade books and children will not become frustrated trying to get sources. However, if you do limit them to a larger content area topic, let children choose their topics within those parameters. If you revisit the study later on, you might let them choose any topic, but it will be more difficult to support them with classroom resources if the topics come from far and wide. In addition, you will need to assemble some books on topics you predict your students might choose that are on or about their reading levels. So if your science unit is on the ocean, you can get books that your students can read on sharks, whales, water pollution, and so on. You'll also need to decide what your topic will be, so you can plan your research and your model writing for the class.

Once again, this is a template of a unit of study, but you will modify it based on your assessment of students' needs.

Day 1

TEACHING POINT One reason writers write about what they read is because they've found something that interests them and they want to tell or teach it to others.

MODEL The teacher models browsing through several books, being intrigued by several topics, and talking about them with a partner.

STUDENTS' WORK FOR THE DAY Students read through the books that the teacher has collected in baskets to find topics of interest.

Day 2

TEACHING POINT When writers have several ideas that interest them, they do more reading to eliminate some topics in favor of the one that will work best for them. (If students have found their topics quickly, an alternative lesson possibility is narrowing the topic itself down to something manageable.)

MODEL The teacher writes his three possibilities, one of which will become the topic he writes about for all modeling, on chart paper. He talks about his plans for narrowing down to one topic, which include seeing how much information is available on each one, whether he thinks he could write something long about it, and whether he already knows anything about the topic.

STUDENTS' WORK FOR THE DAY Students need to narrow down the number of topics they have. By the end of workshop time, they need to have chosen a topic and written it down in their readers notebooks.

Day 3

TEACHING POINT Once writers have identified a topic, they do more work by reading more about it, taking notes, and having conversations with a partner about it, just as students do when they read fiction in reading workshop.

MODEL The teacher models her plans for reading more about her topic, taking notes, and talking to another teacher about it.

STUDENTS' WORK FOR THE DAY Students choose one of the three ways demonstrated (reading more, taking notes, having conversations) to find out more about the topic and do the work to add to their bank of information. If some students chose the same topic, they can meet to talk with each other about the information they've found, even if it means changing partners for a day.

Day 4

TEACHING POINT When writers write about nonfiction reading, they write from the facts they've found and they cite different sources.

MODEL The teacher models taking notes from different sources on adhesive tags and collecting them on pages in the readers notebook labeled with the title and author of the source. Alternatively, teacher might show taking notes on index cards, coding them for later citation, and keeping them together with a rubber band or in a large resealable baggie.

STUDENTS' WORK FOR THE DAY Students should begin to take notes and to record the sources of each piece of information.

Day 5

TEACHING POINT Writers stop to reread and to reflect on the notes they've taken.

MODEL The teacher goes back to reread his notes, which he's written on chart paper. He demonstrates asking himself these questions:

- ❖ What other information do I need?

- ❖ How does this information fit in with other information I have or what I know about the world?

- ❖ What about this excites me?

- ❖ What don't I understand?

Then he writes a reflection about the information on a separate chart paper.

STUDENTS' WORK FOR THE DAY Students reread the notes they've taken and write a reflection on those notes. They can use a T-chart or a separate page in their notebook, or they can write on an eight-by-five-inch index card and insert it into their notebook.

Day 6

TEACHING POINT Writers talk about their topics, their notes, their reflections, and their ideas with others. They use what others say to grow new insights, refine their thinking, and to get ideas for more information they may need.

MODEL The teacher talks about her information with a student partner or another teacher to demonstrate how talking helps make thinking grow.

STUDENTS' WORK FOR THE DAY Students meet with a partner (or small group) to help each other say smart things about the facts they've found, and to help figure out when they need more facts because some parts of their information are sparse.

Day 7

TEACHING POINT Writers reread notes looking for ways to group information together.

MODEL The teacher models moving around his adhesive notes or index cards looking for ways they belong together. He shows four categories emerging, names what they are, and tries to fit most of his note tags into one of the categories. (Be sure one of the categories is not parallel to the others in preparation for Day 8 lesson.)

STUDENTS' WORK FOR THE DAY Students reread their notes looking for ways they can group them, trying to put each one into a category. Students give each category a name and write them in their notebook.

Day 8

TEACHING POINT Writers determine if their categories are parallel or similar to each other and corresponding in some way.

MODEL The teacher has deliberately chosen one category that does not fit in with the others. Thinking out loud, she demonstrates why that category doesn't fit. For example, if she's chosen to write about what different types of work dogs do, her categories might be hunting, retrieving, guide work, and so on, but "how to groom a dog" doesn't fit in, because it doesn't correspond to the others and it's not what work dogs do. For younger students, the teacher might show that if she's writing about dogs, her categories can be general: their history, loyalty, and physical traits, but a category on dogs' paws won't fit, because it's too specific. If she chooses to write about dogs' paws, then she has to write about dogs' ears, noses, and snouts for the categories to be parallel. The teacher models removing one category, and, for older students, thinking of another category to add in its place.

STUDENTS' WORK FOR THE DAY Students reread their categories and talk with their partner to determine if their categories are parallel. If they aren't, students need to figure out how to change them or what new information they'll need to make a new category to replace the one they need to omit.

Day 9

TEACHING POINT Writers determine if more information is needed in any one category and if so, they do more research. They look for balance in their writing.

MODEL The teacher shows that information in one of his categories is too sparse, so he makes plans to get more facts for it.

STUDENTS' WORK FOR THE DAY Students reread their categories and talk with their partner to determine if any of their categories need more information. If so, they need to make plans to get it.

Day 10

TEACHING POINT Writers use their research to come to new understandings or insights about their topic.

MODEL The teacher models how her collection of facts is making her think some new things about her topic. For example, all her facts about dogs make her think they may be smarter than humans, or humans would have a hard time surviving without them, or they deserve citizenship because they contribute so much to society. The way she shapes her insights will help her determine which genre to write in, or if the genre is specified, that will help her determine which conclusion she will eventually include in her writing and how she will write it. (If you are teaching feature articles, this is where you will teach getting an idea for an angle; if you are teaching editorials, you'll emphasize having a strong opinion based on the facts.)

STUDENTS' WORK FOR THE DAY Students reread and talk with their partner to come up with new insights or conclusions. What can they say about their topic after all they've learned? Students write it down in their notebook.

Day 11

TEACHING POINT Writers use mentor texts to help them decide how their writing should go and to give them a sense of the genre they are writing.

MODEL The teacher reads a mentor text together with the class and talks about features of the genre. He makes a chart of the features. (You will have been reading aloud every day from the genre even before the study began to give children a sense of how the genre sounds. You can find report-like writing in *Dig* magazine, feature articles from *Muse*, and editorials in *New Moon*.)

STUDENTS' WORK FOR THE DAY Students read several reports (or articles or editorials) to find their own mentor text. They should keep a copy of their mentor text to study it.

Day 12

TEACHING POINT Writers plan their writing using outlines, charts, or some types of planning page. One type of planning they do is to look over their categories to decide which one will come first.

MODEL The teacher demonstrates planning her writing, using a combination of ways, and talks about the purpose of each type of planning. She orders her categories, explains why, and numbers them.

STUDENTS' WORK FOR THE DAY Students look at their categories and make plans for how their draft will go, especially which category will come first in their report (feature article, or editorial). They should number the categories in the order they'll write about them.

Day 13

TEACHING POINT Writers also order the information within each category in a way that makes their writing clear and fluid. Then each of the categories becomes an organized paragraph.

MODEL The teacher talks through how he will order the information inside one of his categories. It might be chronologically, leaving the most disgusting fact for the end of the paragraph, moving in sequence from the top of the dog's head to the bottom, or whatever makes sense for the topic and type of information. The teacher names the thinking that goes behind the decision to order information and charts this.

STUDENTS' WORK FOR THE DAY Students order the information within each of their categories by manipulating their adhesive notes or index cards. They number the cards so it will be easier to draft.

Day 14

TEACHING POINT Writers draft their paragraphs from their planning pages and their notes.

MODEL The teacher shows how she goes from notes and planning pages to sentences as she drafts.

STUDENTS' WORK FOR THE DAY Looking at their notes and planning pages, students draft their piece.

Day 15

TEACHING POINT Writers use mentor texts to help them write leads.

MODEL The teacher shows how he studied leads from two mentor texts (or more for older students) and how he plays with his lead based on the leads in two or more mentor texts.

STUDENTS' WORK FOR THE DAY Using their mentor text to help them, students write their lead. Students should try their lead at least one other way using some text the teacher used.

Day 16

TEACHING POINT Writers fold in information to get the most from each sentence, or they get the most from extra information, such as quotes, by leading up to them or explaining why they are important.

MODEL The teacher models how to tuck in extra information using appositives, or for older students, how to use quotes effectively by introducing them or explaining their significance.

STUDENTS' WORK FOR THE DAY Students find one place where they can tuck in more information or where they can use a quote effectively.

Day 17

TEACHING POINT Writers use their reflections to help them write conclusions that bring their readers to new understandings based on the facts.

MODEL Going back to earlier written reflection, the teacher demonstrates writing a concluding sentence or paragraph using her written insights.

STUDENTS' WORK FOR THE DAY Students use their reflections to help them write an ending to their piece.

Day 18

TEACHING POINT Writers revise for voice that is appropriate to the genre.

MODEL Using his mentor text, the teacher models using a writing voice that sounds like the genre yet contains his personality. Depending on the genre, it can be objective or chatty, but it should have authority.

STUDENTS' WORK FOR THE DAY Students revise their draft for voice.

Day 19

TEACHING POINT Writers edit for written language conventions of grammar and punctuation.

MODEL Using editing checklist, the teacher models editing her writing so that someone else can read and understand it.

STUDENTS' WORK FOR THE DAY Students edit their piece using the editing checklist and reading it aloud to their partner.

Day 20

TEACHING POINT Writers make plans for sending their writing out into the world and for publishing it within the classroom.

MODEL The teacher talks about ways he plans to send the writing out into the school community. For older children, he may talk about markets, such as *Stone Soup* and *New Moon.*

STUDENTS' WORK FOR THE DAY Students make plans for sending their writing out and talk with their partner about how they'll do that. They reflect on the work they've done, what they've learned, and what they want to know more about as a reader and writer.

Day 21

Celebrate! And begin the next unit of study!

Name _____ Topic _____

As you collect information for your writing (feature article, editorial, informational report, and so on), make a list in the space below. Then reread the information and reflect on it. What do you think about the facts you have collected on your topic?

Facts About My Topic	My Reflections on Each Fact

FIG. 7–4 *Planning sheet for writing in science or social studies*

Summary

Writing about nonfiction reading in the form of feature articles, editorials, reports, and the like is another way students should write about what they read. If we only teach them to write about fiction, we are not getting the most mileage from all the organizing and thinking work we want them to do. Teaching them to identify a passion and how to do research on it is vital. Equally important is teaching them that the facts alone don't make for fascinating reading. They must figure out something new about the world from the facts they have found and teach it to their audience.

Assessment: Evaluating the Work of Writing About Reading

There is no doubt that assessment is the backbone of teaching. Without assessing students' work, we cannot plan curriculum, nor can we tailor our lessons to students' needs. Without assessment, we don't know what and if our students are learning. Without assessment, we are not teaching, but merely assigning activities to children. Without assessment we cannot be thoughtful, responsive professionals. Assessment must begin on the very first day of school and continue every day after that to give us tools to refine our practice and inform the art and the craft of our teaching.

Early in this book, I told the story of my daughter Cheryl making dioramas and writing book reports to prove she'd read books. Her well-intentioned teachers designed these activities because they wanted to be sure students understood what they read. Their intentions were good, and teachers still struggle with how to know whether children are really "getting" what they read and with holding students "accountable" for their reading. Although this book suggests alternative ways for children to write about their reading, we still need some kind of product—conversation, notes, written responses, book reviews—to assess students' understanding of text. The difference is that we are not assigning glitzy or cute activities or asking for writing genres that don't exist in the world. Nevertheless, the products we now ask from children, from notes to literary essays, all should be assessed as evidence of the mind-work children are doing in their reading. And all assessment should inform our instruction (Spandel, 2001), whether it's to teach students to revise or to plan further instruction in using conversations to shape ideas or finding and organizing evidence and so on.

As we rethink the usefulness of book reports and writing letters to book characters and consider replacing them with real-world genres of writing, we want to raise the bar for students and for our own teaching. When we see that students are not learning something we have taught, it is time for us to stop and assess the work we are doing every day in the classroom. As harsh as it seems, we cannot lay blame on students when our teaching isn't good enough to reach them. In addition, when we assess student work, it is largely for the purpose of planning curriculum and assessing the effectiveness of our instruction, rather than handing out grades. And although there is no doubt that teachers must give grades and that they are responsible for giving grades for which they have solid evidence—accountable grading, if you will—grades are not the main reason for assessing student work.

I would suggest that we could use conversation, notes, and readers notebook entries as samples of student writing to assess comprehension and that writing about reading genres should be assessed in terms of genre, organization of ideas, and qualities of good writing. If students have not understood a text, it will be impossible for them to talk or write thoughtfully about it. Therefore the content of students' conversations and writing will demonstrate the depth of their understanding and processing of the text. Assessing whether students have understood the text is not as simple as asking them to retell the plot, because they can do that without actually reading the book—they can see the movie, or ask someone what it's about, or read the book jacket. We want to require students to demonstrate that they have read thoroughly and thoughtfully and attempted to place the text within their literary experience. Students prove understanding by producing some evidence of their thinking, which can range from notes in preparation for conversation to an actual writing piece that charts the reader's work throughout a text. We can assess any combination of these, but we must be sure our criteria are clear to students and to ourselves and that our purpose is to inform our literacy instruction (Cambourne and Turbill, 1994).

In this chapter we will look at how to assess three categories of student products:

◈ the depth and extent of conversations in partnerships, small groups, and whole-class discussions

◈ the amount and quality of students' notes to prepare for talking, writing, and extending ideas, including the use of their readers notebooks

◈ the development of ideas, qualities of good writing, and understanding of genre in longer pieces of writing about reading

We will also examine how writing about reading can prepare children for the statewide reading and writing tests that so many states now require.

The Depth and Extent of Group Conversations

The assessment of student conversation will begin on the first day of school as you observe the interactions of your students. Although children clearly are nervous on the first day, you can begin to get a sense of the dynamics between students. You'll also be able to see what you have to do to establish a safe, risk-free environment (Peterson, 1992). For students who are experienced with community conversations, there will be less work to do; with less experienced students, you'll need to determine what students know and what you need to teach them. Establishing community happens all day long; it is not something you only work on during reading or writing workshop, but it is setting up the way you expect students to act toward each other every day throughout the school year by your own example. So your early assessment will involve anecdotal notes on which students seem to talk or to hold back, which students try to dominate the conversation, and which students need more coaching on exactly what kinds of things they can say.

Although much of the work for writing about reading happens in reading workshop early in the year, the work in writing workshop is equally important. Here you are establishing routines for writing, such as writing every day (Calkins, 1994; Ray, 2001; Fletcher, 2001), keeping a writers notebook (Fletcher, 1996a, 1996b), and direct teaching followed by conferring (Anderson, 2000). Using your own writers notebook, you'll be showing children how writers live by writing things down, and once they've established this habit, it will serve their writing and thinking lives well. You will also reinforce the rhythm of the class routines in both reading and writing: direct whole-class instruction, followed by independent work, during which the teacher works with individuals or small groups.

Once you have established partnerships, you will want to begin more formal assessments by listening regularly to the students' conversations. During the time when students are talking with partners, you can confer with some partnerships (Anderson, 2000), and you can listen to assess, using a checklist such as the one in Figure 8–1. Because we want students to be proactive in their own learning, it might be helpful for them to use the same or a similar checklist to assess their own conversations. Often students need to have something in writing that clearly states your expectations for them. You might ask students to fill out a checklist at the same

Criteria	Good	Acceptable	Needs Work	Notes or Possible Minilessons
Equality of participation				
Amount of preparation for talk				
Facility and ease of conversation				
Quality or depth of ideas				
Amount of reference to text				
Staying on topic or moving off with good reason				
Planning for future work				

FIG. 8–1 *Checklist for assessing partnership or small-group conversations*

time you do so that you can see if and how their perceptions differ from yours. After this, you can talk to children about it and then plan your teaching accordingly.

As you move through your curriculum, you might choose one aspect to assess. For example, if you have done a lot of work with referring to text, you may create a short checklist for assessing that as you listen to conversations. Or if you've worked at length on the content of conversations (see Figure 2–1), then you might spend time assessing the depth of student conversations (Figure 8–2). You can assess the group as a whole, and at

Depth of Facility in Having Conversation for Small Group	Notes	Depth of Content in the Group's Conversation	Notes
Honors each voice in the group		Has a controlling idea	
Moves talk along by using transitional phrases		Refers to text or texts	
Stops to restate where group is if necessary		Goes between texts and idea to develop idea	
Uses language to clarify position		The idea grows over conversation— the talk extends the idea	
Decides when an idea is exhausted and group needs to move on		Idea is clear or the group is working to clarify it	
Has language for disagreeing in acceptable ways		Idea is significant or worth considering; not obvious or literal	
Can determine when to end the conversation		Idea is based on a theme or some idea that goes across texts	
Makes appropriate plans for more talk and reading		Alludes to other texts to build understanding or support stance	

FIG. 8–2 *Checklist for depth in student conversations*

other times assess individuals within the group. It is important to note the sometimes conversational rhythms and language are cultural, so you'll want to respect students' identities while assessing the ways they use language to move their conversations along.

Because it is often difficult to assess every group during reading or writing time, you might ask for students' permission to audiotape a conversation to assess later (check with your district for policy on getting parental permission for audiotaping). Listening to a tape when you can give it full attention can teach you a great deal about what students know and can (or can't) do. You'll be able to hear nuances and subtleties that are lost in the fast pace of live conversation, and these may give you insights that will strengthen your teaching greatly.

For assessing conversations in partnerships, small groups, or the whole class, a checklist may be sufficient if it's based on exactly what you've taught. You might decide not to use this list for grading but just to plan your next steps. If you do intend to use this kind of list for grading, you'd want to discuss it with children first and be sure they understand what you intend to do and exactly what you'll be evaluating.

Carrying a conversation is a social skill, so you want to be sure that if you use the information for grading, it is on the content of what students say, not on their social abilities. You may evaluate conversational ability only if it is to plan how you will coach children to talk in a small group, that is, to plan your teaching, but I think it is not appropriate to grade children on whether or not they are shy or quick-witted.

Listening to students' conversations regularly can give you a wealth of information about what you need to teach and whether it needs to be taught to the whole class, to a small group, or to an individual. In addition, you will want to assess the way each student positions himself as a learner in the workshop. Is he ready to learn from peers and from writers? Is she working to use what she knows about reading to inform her writing? Writing about reading gives us a wonderful opportunity to marry reading and writing together, and we may want to assess how our students are learning from that match.

Amount and Quality of Students' Notes

Because note-taking is crucial to the later longer writing about reading, students need to demonstrate that they can do this. You'll want to think about how to assess this writing, as it will be the first writing about reading that children will do. You might begin by asking students to choose their best adhesive note from the books they are reading and talk about it with you. This could be followed in the next book by choosing the best note and handing it in with a sentence or two about why the student feels it is the best one. For older students, you'll expect more notes sooner and longer reflections on them, ranging from several notes to a larger number on a certain topic (for example, eight to ten notes that show how ideas about one character changed) and reflections ranging from a paragraph to a page. Again, this is what you'd do earlier in the year, because as the year goes on, you'll introduce genres of writing about reading and expect children to write in those.

Once partnerships and small-group conversations have been established, it is fair to expect that students will hand in some kind of writing for many if not most of the books they read, although I would caution against requiring writing about all the books they read. I would also offer students a choice about which kind of writing they want to hand you for a given book, while expecting that there will be a set number of longer pieces required across the year. Obviously, the longer writing will tend to appear in the second half of the year, because that is when you are focusing on it. But notes and a reflection should still be part of how some children respond, even after you have taught, say, literary essays. You just wouldn't expect children to write literary essays about every book, nor does every book deserve the effort and time of an essay. Here is a possible menu for what you might require of students, although I would require more of older students and less of less experienced students. I've included an alternative plan in the form of a letter to students.

Menu for Writing About Reading Across the Year Based on Twenty-Five Books Per Year

one literary essay from genre study, plus one additional independent essay

two author profiles of authors of your choice

one book review from genre study, plus four additional book reviews

three long entries from readers notebook for each of eight books

four or five adhesive notes with written reflections and planning
   pages for longer writing for each of eight books

Dear students,

For most of the books you read, you will be asked to hand in some kind of writing. I'll expect you to read at least twenty-five books this year, and you will be required to write about twenty of those twenty-five books. If you read fewer books, please talk to me about the number of writings required. Most of the time, you will be able to choose which books you'll write about, although sometimes I will ask you to definitely write about a certain book, such as our read-aloud.

Below is a list of the kinds of writing you can do and hand in for evaluation. You should choose a different type of writing for each book and be able to say why you chose one type of writing over another.

- one adhesive note or index card

- several notes with observations or reflections on the thinking they show

- short responses or reflections, either flagged in your readers notebook or taken out of the notebook and extended on a separate sheet

- notes, graphic organizers, charts, and plans for longer writing

- full pieces of writing about reading in genres we will study

- at least one independent try in a genre after we have studied it

One major way to assess student work is to confer with students as they are writing. Carl Anderson (2000) tells us that we can teach into students' intentions as they write, helping them to grow as writers and thinkers. As you meet with individual students, ask each one what he is trying to accomplish as a writer. How is she trying to get her ideas as a reader into her writing? How can he use the qualities of good writing he's learned to help him write clearly about his reading? How do her notes and plans help her to say what she wants to say?

In a conference, you want to teach the writer something new or coach him to do something he wants to do as a writer, but doesn't yet know how. Later you can revisit that child and see to what extent he followed the direct teaching you did in your conference with him. You will probably have reading conferences with him to teach him strategies for reading, and you will also have writing conferences, where you will teach him how to write well about the ideas he had in his reading. The notes you take in these conferences will prove invaluable as you plan individual and group teaching and as you evaluate students' work.

One way to evaluate notes students have taken in their readers notebooks is to consider how these notes helped the child prepare for longer writing. Sometimes students' notes will be obvious, or random, or contain information that they do not develop when they write longer pieces. Although it is unrealistic to expect that every note taken will feed later writing, it is sensible that longer writing should grow from notes. These notes are germinating ideas, which then must be nurtured to grow into longer and larger pieces.

You might use the following short rubric in Figure 8–3 to assess student notes that you require as the first work in a longer piece of writing or as evidence of thinking during reading.

Name _____   Book Title _____

Notes Are:	Most of the Time	Sometimes	Rarely
Notes are clear and legible.			
Notes are short: uses phrases.			
Notes are short: uses abbreviations.			
Notes are short: uses arrows and symbols.			
Notes attempt to capture a significant idea.			
Notes record evidence to build or support an idea.			
Notes appear to have a rationale behind taking them.			

FIG. 8–3 *Rubric for assessing notes in student writing about reading*

You might also collect students' readers notebooks regularly to see what work they are doing. Ask them to flag an entry they want you to read, or read through all the pages to get a sense of how the notebook is helping thinking and preparation for longer writing. I would caution you against responding to the children in these notebooks, lest the purpose change from recording reading insights to teacher–student dialogue journals. Like writers notebooks, readers notebooks have a specific purpose. They allow readers to collect their thinking and the evidence behind it in preparation for conversation and/or longer writing. They are not to establish a written dialogue with the teacher. Although you might wish to have this type of written interaction with students too, I would suggest doing it in separate notebooks for that purpose. Certainly the content in the notebooks will be something about which you'll want to confer with them.

Anne, a sixth grader, began by taking notes on adhesives in the book she was reading, *Artemis Fowl* by Eoin Colter. *Artemis Fowl* is a fantasy book set in Ireland about a young boy genius who schemes to kidnap a fairy and steal the fairy kingdom's gold. For a final project, Anne collected five of the notes that traced her thinking about the book, as well as two notebook entries that showed her thinking path. Anne pushed herself to find significant meaning inside an entertaining and deceptively obvious plot. Although there are many things she could have written about, especially in terms of the book being a typical fantasy, Anne chose a rather serious idea to investigate. She worked to find evidence in the book and to include it in her essay, which she handed in along with her notes and notebook entries. Anne's work shows she not only had a literal understanding of the story, but also that she used her teacher's instruction about characters to build a deeper knowledge. Anne's writing demonstrates taking an idea, growing it, and showing how that idea exists in the world beyond the book (Figure 8–4). It is thoughtful and solid and demonstrates what her teacher hoped students would be able to do with any book.

One way to evaluate notes is to ask students to assemble several notes about a single idea and to highlight where those notes helped form their thinking or advance their planning for longer writing. One reason this is helpful is that it teaches students to evaluate their own work (Greene, 1994) by rereading and choosing notes for the teacher's assessment. In terms of requirements for publishing written pieces, I would not accept published writing that did not have a history behind it in terms of notes, reflections, planning pages, and drafts. Although you might vary the amount of prewriting that you require children to submit, it is probably

A - not really as mean as wants to be

p. 122

A - like adult b/c must take care of mom/ Dad is gone.

A - man of the house

p. 21

A - lack of emotion b/c hurts too much (mom is crazy)

p. 117

Spys on mom like parents spy on kids - for their own good

He is parent

p. 142

A - like a bully - pretends to be tough
- wants a family + love (like Crash)
- gave up $ for love

p. 276

A = Artemis

FIG. 8–4a *Anne's notes*

unsafe to accept work that does not have the legitimacy of planning work behind it. Many children understand that it is the process of writing that we need to evaluate, not just the product, but those who don't might be tempted at times to find writing elsewhere and submit it as their own. Of course, this is unfortunate, but we can forestall this by asking for the supporting "documents" so we can study students' thinking and planning.

Development of Ideas, Qualities of Good Writing, and Understanding of Genre

If writing about reading is done to demonstrate the thinking students have done about a text, then it makes sense to evaluate the development of ideas as part of their work. Although we all hope children will have deep

Artemis Fowl

Artemis Fowl likes to appear tough and clever to Butler, Juliet, and the fairies. Sometimes he seems to be really mean and cruel but I think he isn't really because he almost cries when he sees his mother is crazy. At the end, he gives up some of his money that he worked so hard for so he can make his mom better again. If he really was a mean guy who had no feelings, he would have kept all the money. Also, when he thinks his dad is back with his mom, he starts to get excited, but when he finds out it isn't true, he starts to cry. He just hides his emotions from other people but the reader can see that he isn't all bad.

Artemis reminds me of my brother who is really smart and kids always make fun of him and call him a nerd. He has no friends and spends most of his free time in front of the computer or playing video games so he is really pale. Sometimes when I talk to him he gets very condescending and know it all like Artemis. But I think he does that because he feels bad about not having friends and being cool and being smart is the only weapon he has. If he can feel smarter than everyone else, then he can feel better about himself—he doesn't need other people. Artemis does the same thing, especially when he talks to the fairies. He assumes that they are not as smart as he is.

In the book, *Artemis Fowl* by Eion Colfer, Artemis Fowl appears to be a very mean 12 year old boy who only cares about cheating the fairies out of their money so he can be rich. But after reading the book, I believe that Artemis isn't really as mean and uncaring as he seems at first. He hides his feelings because they hurt too much and because it makes him seem more like an adult. He needs to feel like a grownup because his parents aren't there to take care of him.

In one part of the book, Artemis spies on his mom through a hidden camera in her room. He feels guilty about spying but he wants to make sure she is ok because she is kind of crazy and hears voices. Artemis is like the parent and his mom is the kid. Sometimes parents spy on their kids for their own good. This is what he does to his mom.

Since Artemis' dad is gone and his mom is sick, he doesn't have parents who can love him and take care of him. That is why he has to act so tough and like an adult. Deep down inside, he wants to have a family that loves him even if it means that he can't have as much freedom. In the beginning of the book, he likes having freedom but in the end he gives away half of his money he worked so hard for. He would rather have his mom all better than have money. When she is healed, he regrets loosing his freedom but he is happy because he has a mom and her love. Artemis is like Crash Coogan the bully in *Crash* because he acts like a bully in order to hide his true feelings that he wants a loving, happy family.

Many kids act mean or tough on the outside because then other people can't make fun of them for what they really feel. Maybe if Artemis had a nice family and some good friends then he would be able to make more jokes and use his genius for doing good deeds instead of crime.

FIG. 8–4b *Anne's writing*

insights about reading, it is equally important that they demonstrate using this "process," or that they show they read actively to find literal and inferential meaning in a text. Furthermore, if we agree that there is no one interpretation of a text, then students are free to construct any idea, providing they can find proof in the text.

If students have taken clear and careful notes, preparing to write longer pieces would not be so daunting for them. Once you have taught students to write in various genres, you'll want to evaluate how their note-taking helped their thinking, but you'll also want to evaluate their understanding of the genre. Part of this is assessing their understanding of genre study in general (Cooper, 1999), and for that you might have a general rubric that you use for any genre unit of study in your writing instruction (Figure 8–5). However, you may decide that you want to assess the genre more specifically, in which case you could construct a rubric based on the actual lessons you taught during the study. For example, if in a book review unit of study you emphasized the tone and language of book reviews, then you would assess students on that; if, however, you emphasize writing a summary into

Criteria	Most of the Time	Sometimes	Rarely
Shows thorough notes to prepare for writing			
Includes a planning page of some kind			
Includes a reflection			
Includes one or more drafts			
Shows some revisions			
Has edited for written conventions of grammar, punctuation, and spelling			
Demonstrates an understanding of the characteristics of the genre			
Shows the use of a mentor text			

FIG. 8–5 *Rubric for any genre unit of study*

the reviews, then you would assess that. Whatever you have taught is the criteria that you will add to your rubric, because it is reasonable to expect that students can produce what you've taught (Figure 8–6).

It is important to remember that your assessment of student work must directly reflect your teaching, and that it is unfair to assess students on strategies you have not actually taught to them. On the other hand, whatever you do teach them should be evaluated in some way (Ray, 2001) and should

Criteria	Most of the Time	Sometimes	Rarely
States book title(s) and author			
Gives background info (awards, previous book, and so on)			
Includes a carefully written summary that names characters and problem or topic of the book (nonfiction)			
States reviewer's opinion in objective language			
Highlights some part of text			
Includes a telling quote and elaborates on it			
Opens with a catchy statement			
Writes with authority			
Includes advice to the reader			
Leaves us with a sense of whether or not to read this book			

FIG. 8–6 *Rubric for book review unit of study: items added to general rubric*

appear on a clear rubric that communicates your expectations to students (Falk, 2000). Students should also be given an opportunity to evaluate themselves based on the work you've done with them (Figure 8–7).

Name Constanza Arnes Cruz November 26, 2002

Literary Essay Reflection

Do you think you did enough work in your Reader's Notebook before beginning your essay? Describe the work you did.

I think that I did enough work thinking about the essay, getting the gist of the body paragraphs and working out what the story is really about

Are you pleased with your thesis statement? Explain why or why not.

Broken Sky is the kind of book that doesn't have a very clear message so it was hard for me to find a thesis. But I am pleased with it.

Describe something you had a hard time with in your essay.

I had a hard time finding a thesis statement and finding examples.

What are you most proud of in your essay? Describe what you did.

I am most proud of the fact that I went over my essay last night and I helped it to become much better.

Literary Essay Editing Checklist

Editing Reminders for Formal Writing:

Did you make sure you used the 3rd person? ➤ No "I." ("I" is the 1st person.)	✓
Did you use the present tense? ➤ This story *is* about.... (Not: This story *was* about....) ➤ India Opal *brings* the people in the town closer together. (Not: India Opal *brought* the people in the town closer together.)	✓
Did you make sure you didn't use any slang or conversational language? ➤ No "You know what I mean?"	✓
Did you make sure you didn't use any contractions? ➤ Write "is not" instead of "isn't," etc.	✓

Other Editing Reminders:

Did you underline the title of your book?	✓
Did you capitalize the author's name?	✓
Are all words spelled correctly?	✓
Is there a title to the essay? Does the title hint at what the thesis is?	✓
Is there a period, question mark, or exclamation mark at the end of every sentence?	✓
Is each paragraph indented?	✓
Did you use quotation marks for quotes taken directly from the text?	✓
Is there a capital letter at the beginning of every sentence?	✓

Typing Reminders:

➤ Use *Times New Roman* font.
➤ Use size 14.
➤ Use double-spacing.

Name ______________________ Date __________

Literary Essay Revision Checklists

Introduction Paragraph

Do you tell the title (underlined) and author of the book?	✓
Do you give some background information about the story?	✓
Do you mention the main character?	✓
Do you have a thesis sentence?	✓
Do all sentences make sense?	✓
Are all sentences self-explanatory? Do all sentences follow the assumption that the reader of your essay has not read the book?	✓

Body Paragraphs For each of your 3 (or more) body paragraphs...

Do you have a topic sentence that is connected to your thesis?	✓	✓	✓
Does your topic sentence make a smooth transition from the paragraph before?	✓	✓	✓
Do you give quotes or examples from the book?	✓	✓	✓
Do you explain why the quotes or examples connect to your thesis?	✓	✓	✓
Do you have a clincher sentence?	✓	✓	✓
Do all sentences make sense?	✓	✓	✓
Are all sentences self-explanatory? Do all sentences follow the assumption that the reader of your essay has not read the book?	✓	✓	✓

Conclusion Paragraph

Do you restate your thesis?	✓
Do you summarize the evidence from your body paragraphs?	✓
Do you suggest some new thinking about the book? Leave the reader to think about how the thesis relates to the real world. Make a reference back to who wrote the book or what the main character teaches us. Invite or encourage others to want to read the book or look further into the subject.	✓
Do all sentences make sense?	✓
Are all sentences self-explanatory? Do all sentences follow the assumption that the reader of your essay has not read the book?	✓

FIG. 8–7 *Student evaluation*

Many states have instituted assessments at various grades that attempt to determine how students are progressing in reading and writing. Ultimately, the intention of these tests is to evaluate instruction, but, of course, as teachers we want our students to do well because we know what these tests mean for them as learners. There is no doubt in my mind that the best preparation for any statewide assessment of reading and writing is daily, solid, direct, and individual instruction in reading and writing and a substantial block of time to practice every day. Students who read and write every day in school will have a much better chance of doing well on these tests.

For these reasons, I agree with Lucy Calkins, Kate Montgomery, and Donna Santman (1998), who write in their book *A Teacher's Guide to Standardized Tests* that art projects and letters to dead authors do not help children interact with texts in bold, vigorous ways. We need children to get their minds working, so that when they are faced with a passage to read and interpret on a test, they have done that many times. When they must read and comprehend selections in various genres, they've done this many times. And when they must synthesize what they've read and produce some writing about it in an organized way, they have done this many times.

Teaching children to read carefully and thoughtfully is essential to their performance on these assessments, and teaching them to take notes from their reading and to organize, plan, and execute writing is what enhances their performance. I want to emphasize that we do not teach children to write about reading only to pass these tests, nor is this the only type of writing that I want them to do in school—we need personal narratives, poetry, editorials, sports writing, and so on for children to have a varied writing diet. But the work of writing about reading is uniquely suited to what children are required to produce on these tests: appropriate note-taking, evidence of planning for writing, having and developing a clear idea, and use of evidence from the text, as well as all the qualities of good writing you would have taught them all year. Unfortunately, writing book reports and making bookmarks won't teach this, nor will endless work on prompted writing.

Children must be able to interact with texts and trust that they can put down their ideas on paper. If they learn to do this and they do it regularly about books they have chosen to read, they will have more than adequate preparation for the kind of writing they will do on these tests. A week or two before the test should be spent familiarizing them with how the test will look, as well as how they can take all they know about writing and use it on the test. Students should do well if they are used to reading carefully and accurately, taking notes, and using their notes to produce coherent writing.

Summary

For writing about reading to be more than a new variation on asking children to prove they've read their books, we must use the writing to inform our teaching, as well as to teach children that readers really do write about what they read. When we assess student writing about reading, it is partially to see what students have learned, but just as much to see what we need to reteach. Reflective teachers will use assessment as a way to evaluate their own teaching and to think about what went well and what can be changed. Ultimately, we want children to learn so they can perform independently, and we want to be the most effective teachers possible.

Conclusion

Final Thoughts:
Changing Students as Readers Forever

I'm sitting in a third-grade classroom in Connecticut, but I could be in any classroom, anywhere in the country. All around me, children are looking between their books and their notes, and they are writing about their books on adhesive notes, in notebooks, on charts, and in drafts of longer pieces. As I think about these children and their work, I wonder how many of them will continue to be readers and writers long after their teacher and I leave them, how many of them will make writing about reading part of their literate lives. Looking at these students, I know there is a good chance of that happening. I am relieved, because I know that much of the writing they will be called upon to do in their school and working lives will be in response to something they've read, whether it's facts, statistics, or the latest book.

One of the most important things I've learned from Lucy Calkins, founding director of the Teachers College Reading and Writing Project, is that our teaching should change students' lives forever. At one of our Thursday think tank meetings, she said, "How will your teaching matter to them for the next day and the next day and the day after that? What difference will it make to them next year?" Her words changed *my teaching* forever. I saw that I only had one hundred and eighty days to make a lasting mark on children's lives, only one hundred and eighty opportunities to teach them reading and writing lessons that would stay with them forever. And I realized with shocking clarity that there was no time to waste, that every precious minilesson had to do a lot of work.

It is a huge responsibility, this profession of teaching. We are called to teach every day in powerful ways that matter, and this charge requires that we be at our smartest every day. We must prepare insightful, precise, direct instruction every day. Our lessons must be clear, wise, and specific, and our conferring with individuals and small groups tailored to their exact needs. We must not only consider what to teach, but also *how* to teach it, how to choose the exact words to teach them what we want them to learn. When we teach children to write about their reading—novels, biographies, poetry, science texts, articles, and so on—it must be the very best teaching we can do. And assigning book reports is not our very best teaching.

Book reports do not change lives. At their best, book reports tell the teacher that the student read the book—maybe. They may only tell that the student read the jacket, or skimmed the book, or saw the film, or asked his brother about it. Because the purpose of book reports is to check up on their comprehension, they do not deliver the needed information beyond the shadow of a doubt. A teacher can be no surer that a child read a book by reading a book report than he is with a mobile, bookmark, or diorama.

But writing that prepares a child for long conversations, that grows from careful and thorough notes, or that comes from yearning to say something about a text in a letter or review *does* show whether or not the child has read the book. You cannot talk and write coherently and deeply about a book you haven't read and understood. You *must* have "gotten it" to have something original and insightful to say.

Teachers, we can tell by their eyes if they are "fudging it," because no one can talk for long about something he knows nothing about. It's like the conversations I try to have with my family about Robert Jordan's books. I haven't read them, so I stammer and rely on the book jackets. But they just laugh at me and my pitiful efforts. I just can't pull it off. I have nothing intelligent to say. And it shows.

Our best teaching requires that we raise the bar for students so they do the very best work with the books they read, not the minimum. How much easier, almost offensively so, is it to make a mobile or scribble a few paragraphs that say little beyond a quick retelling and whether they liked the book? It's as if we were telling them we know reading and thinking are too hard for them, so we'll let them off the hook with some drawing. This is not to say that children cannot respond with great depth through art, but often that's not what we're requiring or getting. Often we get weak substitutes for the intelligent responses we want. If we're not asking the best from students, then we're not doing our best teaching. We owe it to our communities to require more, both from our students and from ourselves.

When Cheryl was in school, she realized quickly that her reading life did not match her teacher's expectations. She learned to play the game of book response in school: safe, inane book reports, pretty dioramas, and sequined bookmarks. She kept her teachers happy, because they asked so little of her. She could and would have done much more, had they asked. In her "underground" reading life, she was writing adaptations of books for her dolls to act out, writing letters to camp friends about the heartbreak of the latest book she'd read, writing indictments of Katherine Paterson for writing too-painful stories, planning what she'd say if she could interview Judy Blume. None of this showed up in school; it remained her secret literary life. All her teachers knew and said was that Cheryl didn't read enough because she hadn't written enough book reports. How sad and short-sighted. How tragic that Cheryl couldn't trust her teachers with the truth of her reading life for fear the teachers wouldn't understand.

For sure, Cheryl was an unusual child. She had a vivid imagination and a passion for literature that is even stronger now that she is a woman in her twenties. To this day, she writes about what she reads in ways that astound me with their depth and length, long missives about the need to read this book *now*, letters to Renaissance scholars about their latest research, chapters of a fantasy novel based on her medieval studies, a libretto for an opera about women mystics. She's figured out that literate people read all the time and that they can't help but muse and use what they've read. And all that musing leads them to do some writing. It's just what readers do.

I don't doubt that what Cheryl figured out to do on her own, other children do on their own or could do if they were shown how. Most students are waiting eagerly for us to just tell them what to do. They come to school not really knowing what it's all about, but too often they learn very quickly it's not about much.

What have we taught and how will it affect them forever? The ways our students talk and write about texts, the ways the voices of their hearts are changed, will show us exactly how effective our teaching has been. We owe it to ourselves to make it the smartest work we ever do.

Bibliography

Anderson, Carl. 2000. *How's It Going? A Practical Guide to Conferring with Student Writers*. Portsmouth, NH: Heinemann.

Anderson, Laurie Halse. 1999. *Speak*. New York: Farrar, Straus and Giroux.

Angelillo, Janet. 2002. *A Fresh Approach to Teaching Punctuation*. New York: Scholastic.

Anthony, Robert J., Terry D. Johnson, Norma I. Mickelson, and Alison Preece. 1991. *Evaluating Literacy: A Perspective for Change*. Portsmouth, NH: Heinemann.

Barzun, Jacques. 2001. *Simple and Direct*, 4th ed. New York: Quill.

Barzun, Jacques, and Henry F. Graff. 1992. *The Modern Researcher*, 5th ed. London: Wadsworth.

Beach, Richard. 1993. *A Teacher's Introduction to Reader Response Theories*. Urbana, IL: NCTE.

———. 1999. "Evaluating Students' Response Strategies in Writing about Literature." In Charles R. Cooper and Lee Odell, eds. *Evaluating Writing*. Urbana, IL: NCTE.

Berthoff, Ann E. 1981. *The Making of Meaning*. Portsmouth, NH: Boynton Cook.

Bettleheim, Bruno. 1985. *The Uses of Enchantment: The Uses and Importance of Fairy Tales*. New York: Random House.

Bomer, Randy, and Katherine Bomer. 2001. *For a Better World: Reading and Writing for Social Action*. Portsmouth, NH: Heinemann.

Booth, Wayne C., Gregory C. Colomb, and Joseph M. Williams. 1995. *The Craft of Research*. Chicago: University of Chicago Press.

Britton, James. 1993. *Language and Learning*, 2nd ed. Portsmouth, NH: Heinemann.

Calkins, Lucy McCormick. 1994. *The Art of Teaching Writing*, 2nd ed. Portsmouth, NH: Heinemann.

———. 2001. *The Art of Teaching Reading*. New York: Addison Wesley.

Calkins, Lucy, and Shelley Harwayne. 1991. *Living Between the Lines*. Portsmouth, NH: Heinemann.

Calkins, Lucy, Kate Montgomery, and Donna Santman. 1998. *A Teacher's Guide to Standardized Tests: Knowledge is Power*. Portsmouth, NH: Heinemann.

Cambourne, Brian, and Jan Turbill, eds. 1994. *Responsive Evaluation: Making Valid Judgments about Student Literacy*. Portsmouth, NH: Heinemann.

Clements, Andrew. 1998. *Frindle*. New York: Simon & Schuster.

Coman, Carolyn. 1995. *What Jamie Saw*. Arden, NC: Front Street.

Cooper, Charles R. 1999. "What We Know about Genres, and How It Can Help Us Assign and Evaluate Writing." In Charles R. Cooper and Lee Odell, eds. *Evaluating Writing*. Urbana, IL: NCTE.

Creech, Sharon. 1994. *Walk Two Moons*. New York: Harper Collins.

Daniels, Harvey. 1994. *Literature Circles: Voice and Choice in the Student-Centered Classroom*. York, ME: Stenhouse.

Falk, Beverly. 2000. *The Heart of the Matter: Using Standards and Assessment to Learn*. Portsmouth, NH: Heinemann.

Fletcher, Ralph. 1996a. *Breathing In, Breathing Out*. Portsmouth, NH: Heinemann.

———. 1996b. *The Writer's Notebook*. New York: Avon Books.

———. 1998. *Flying Solo*. New York, Clarion.

Fletcher, Ralph, and Joann Portalupi. 2001. *Writing Workshop: The Essential Guide*. Portsmouth, NH: Heinemann.

Flynn, Nick, and Shirley McPhillips. 1999. *A Note Slipped Under the Door: Teaching from Poems We Love*. Portland, ME: Stenhouse.

Fountas, Irene, and Gay Su Pinnell. 1996. *Guided Reading: Good First Teaching for All Children*. Portsmouth, NH: Heinemann.

———. 1999. *Matching Books to Readers: Using Leveled Books in Guided Reading K–3*. Portsmouth, NH: Heinemann.

———. 2001. *Guiding Readers and Writers (Grades 3–6): Teaching Comprehension, Genre, and Content Literacy*. Portsmouth, NH: Heinemann.

Greene, Maxine. 1994. "Children as Evaluators: Understanding Evaluation from the Inside." In Brian Cambourne and Jan Turbill, eds. *Responsive Evaluation: Making Valid Judgments about Student Literacy*. Portsmouth, NH: Heinemann.

Hansen, Jane. 1998. *When Learners Evaluate*. Portsmouth, NH: Heinemann.

Harvey, Stephanie. 1998. *Nonfiction Matters: Reading, Writing, and Research in Grades 3–8*. York, ME: Stenhouse.

Harvey, Stephanie, and Anne Goudvis. 2000. *Strategies That Work: Teaching Comprehension to Enhance Understanding*. York, ME: Stenhouse.

Harwayne, Shelley. 1992. *Lasting Impressions*. Portsmouth, NH: Heinemann.

Henkes, Kevin. 1997. *Sun and Spoon*. New York: Greenwillow.

Keene, Ellin, and Susan Zimmerman. 1997. *Mosaic of Thought: Teaching Comprehension in a Reader's Workshop*. Portsmouth, NH: Heinemann.

Krashen, Stephen. 1993. *The Power of Reading: Insights from the Research*. Englewood, CO: Libraries Unlimited, Inc.

Langer, Judith. 1995. *Envisioning Literature: Literary Understanding and Literature Instruction*. New York: Teachers College Press.

Lowry, Lois. 1989. *Number the Stars*. Boston: Houghton Mifflin.

MacLachlan, Patricia. 1995. *What You Know First*. New York: HarperCollins.

Maxim, Donna. 1998. "Nonfiction Literature as the 'Text' of My Intermediate Classroom: That's a Fact." In Rosemary A. Bamford and Janice V. Kristo, eds. *Making Facts Come Alive*. Norwood, MA: Christopher-Gordon Publishers.

Murray, Donald M. 1996. *Crafting a Life: In Essay, Story, Poem*. Portsmouth, NH: Heinemann.

———. 1999. *Write to Learn*. Portsmouth, NH: Heinemann.

Naylor, Phyllis Reynolds. 1991. *Shiloh*. New York: Atheneum.

Newkirk, Thomas, and Patricia McLure. 1992. *Listening In: Children Talk about Books (and Other Things)*. Portsmouth, NH: Heinemann.

Nia, Isoke. 1999. "Units of Study in the Writing Workshop." *Primary Voices K–6* (8) 1.

Paterson, Katherine. 1977. *Bridge to Terabithia*. New York: Harper & Row.

———. 1978. *The Great Gilly Hopkins*. New York: Crowell.

Peterson, Ralph. 1992. *Life in a Crowded Place*. Portsmouth, NH: Heinemann.

Philbrick, Rodman. 1993. *Freak the Mighty*. New York: Blue Sky Press, Scholastic.

Portalupi, Joann, and Ralph Fletcher. 2001. *Nonfiction Craft Lessons: Teaching Information Writing K–8*. Portland, ME: Stenhouse.

———. 2001. *Writing Workshop: The Essential Guide*. Portsmouth, NH: Heinemann.

Probst, Robert. 1987. *Response and Analysis*. Portsmouth, NH: Boynton Cook.

Ray, Katie Wood. 1999. *Wondrous Words: Writers and Writing in the Elementary Classroom*. Urbana, IL: NCTE.

———. 2001. *The Writing Workshop: Working Through the Hard Parts (And They're All Hard Parts)*. Urbana, IL: NCTE.

———. 2002. *What You Know By Heart: How to Develop Curriculum for Your Writing Workshop*. Portsmouth, NH: Heinemann.

Robb, Laura. 2000. *Teaching Reading in a Middle School*. New York: Scholastic.

Rogoff, Barbara. 1990. *Apprenticeship in Thinking: Cognitive Development in Social Context*. New York: Oxford University Press.

Rogovin, Paula. 2001. *The Research Workshop: Bringing the World into Your Classroom*. Portsmouth, NH: Heinemann.

Rosenblatt, Louise. 1995. *Literature as Exploration*, 5th ed. New York: Modern Language Association.

Ryan, Pam Munoz. 2000. *Esperanza Rising*. New York: Scholastic.

Rylant, Cynthia. 1998. *Scarecrow*. San Diego: Harcourt Brace.

Sachar, Louis. 1998. *Holes*. New York: Farrar, Straus and Giroux.

Short, Kathy G., Jerome C. Harste, and Carolyn Burke. 1996. *Creating Classrooms for Authors and Inquirers,* 2nd ed. Portsmouth, NH: Heinemann.

Short, Kathy Gnagey, and Kathryn Mitchell Pierce. 1990. *Talking About Books: Creating Literate Communities.* Portsmouth, NH: Heinemann.

Siu-Runyan, Yvonne. 1998. "Writing Nonfiction: Helping Students Teach Others What They Know." In Rosemary A. Bamford and Janice V. Kristo, eds. *Making Facts Come Alive.* Norwood, MA: Christopher-Gordon Publishers.

Smith, Frank. 1988. *Joining the Literacy Club: Further Essays into Education.* Portsmouth, NH: Heinemann.

———. 1998. *The Book of Learning and Forgetting.* New York: Teachers College Press.

Smith, Robert Kimmel. 1984. *The War with Grandpa.* New York: Delacorte.

Spandel, Vicki. 2001. *Creating Writers Through 6-Trait Writing Assessment and Instruction.* New York: Addison Wesley Longman.

Spinelli, Jerry. 1997. *Crash.* New York: Random House.

Stead, Tony. 2002. *Is That a Fact? Teaching Nonfiction Writing K–3.* Portland, ME: Stenhouse.

Strunk, William, and E. B. White. 1979. *The Elements of Style,* 3rd ed. New York: Macmillan.

Taylor, Mildred. 1976. *Roll of Thunder, Hear My Cry.* New York: Dial Books.

Tierney, Robert J., Mark A. Carter, and Laura E. Desai. 1991. *Portfolio Assessment in the Reading-Writing Classroom.* Norwood, MA: Christopher-Gordon Publishers.

Wells, Gordon. 1986. *The Meaning Makers: Children Learning Language and Using Language to Learn.* Portsmouth, NH: Heinemann.

White, E. B. *Charlotte's Web.* 1952. New York: Harper & Row.

Williams, Joseph M. 2000. *Style: Ten Lessons in Clarity and Grace.* New York: Addison Wesley Longman.

Woodson, Jacqueline. 2001. *The Other Side.* New York: Putnam.

Yolen, Jane. 1987. *Owl Moon.* New York: Philomel.

Zinsser, William. 1995. *On Writing Well: An Informal Guide to Writing Nonfiction,* 5th ed. New York: HarperCollins.

List of Recommended Children's Books

There is great variation in what books may be appropriate for one class or another. I strongly urge teachers to read any books before choosing them as read aloud or book club selections. If teachers are adding books to class-room libraries for independent reading, I suggest reading, or at least skimming, them as well. A book may be a fine work of children's or young adult literature, but not appropriate for your class or community. On the other hand, it is rewarding to discover gems and to insert them as key texts in any literacy program.

Almond, David. *Kit's Wilderness*. 1999. New York: Delacorte.

Anderson, Laurie Halse. 2000. *Fever 1793*. New York: Simon & Schuster.

Avi. 2002. *Crispen: The Cross of Lead*. New York: Hyperion.

Babbitt, Natalie. 1975. *Tuck Everlasting*. New York: Farrar, Straus and Giroux.

Choi, Sook Nyul. 1991. *The Year of Impossible Goodbyes*. New York: Houghton Mifflin.

Conly, Jane Leslie. 1993. *Crazy Lady*. New York: HarperCollins.

Couloumbis, Audrey. 1999. *Getting Near to Baby*. New York: G. P. Putnam's Sons.

Creech, Sharon. 2002. *Ruby Holler*. New York: HarperCollins.

———. 1994. *Walk Two Moons*. New York: HarperCollins.

———. 2000. *The Wanderer*. New York: HarperCollins.

Curtis, Christopher Paul. 1999. *Bud, Not Buddy*. New York: Delacorte.

———. 1995. *The Watsons Go to Birmingham*. New York: Delacorte.

Cushman, Karen. 2003. *Rodzina*. New York: Houghton Mifflin.

DiCamillo, Kate. 2000. *Because of Winn Dixie*. Cambridge, MA: Candlewick.

———. 2001. *The Tiger Rising*. Cambridge, MA: Candlewick.

English, Karen. 1999. *Francie*. New York: Farrar, Straus and Giroux.

Fleischman, Sid. 1989. *The Whipping Boy*. New York: Cornerstone.

Fletcher, Ralph. 1998. *Flying Solo*. New York: Clarion.

———. 1995. *Fig Pudding*. New York: Bantam Doubleday Dell.

Funke, Cornelia. 2002. *The Thief Lord*. New York: Scholastic.

Gaiman, Neil. 2002. *Coraline*. New York: HarperCollins.

Giff, Patricia Reilly. 1997. *Lily's Crossing*. New York: Delacorte.

Grimes, Nikki. 2002. *Bronx Masquerade*. New York: Dial Books.

Henkes, Kevin. 1997. *Sun and Spoon*. New York: Greenwillow.

———. 1992. *Words of Stone*. New York: Greenwillow.

Hesse, Karen. 1997. *Out of the Dust*. New York: Schoalstic.

———. 2001. *Witness*. New York: Scholastic.

Hiassen, Carl. 2002. *Hoot*. New York: Alfred A. Knopf.

Holt, Kimberly Willis. 1999. *When Zachary Beaver Came to Town*. New York: Henry Holt.

Horvath, Polly. 2001. *Everything on a Waffle*. New York: Farrar, Straus and Giroux.

Lowry, Lois. 1980. *Autumn Street*. Boston, Houghton Mifflin.

———. 2000. *Gathering Blue*. New York: Houghton Mifflin.

———. 1993. *The Giver*. Boston: Houghton Mifflin.

———. 1989. *Number the Stars*. Boston: Houghton Mifflin.

MacLachlan, Patricia. 1991. *Journey*. New York: Delacorte.

Napoi, Donna Jo. 2002. *Beast*. New York: Atheneum.

———. 2002. *Daughter of Venice*. New York: Random House.

———. 1997. *Stones in Water*. New York: Dutton.

Park, Linda Sue. 2001. *A Single Shard*. New York: Clarion.

Paterson, Katherine. 1977. *Bridge to Terabithia*. New York: Harper & Row.

———. 1978. *The Great Gilly Hopkins*. New York: Crowell.

Paulsen, Gary. 1987. *Hatchet*. New York: Viking Penguin.

———. 1984. *Tracker*. Scarsdale, NY: Bradbury Press.

Peck, Richard. 1998. *Long Way from Chicago*. New York: Dial Books.

———. 2000. *Year Down Yonder*. New York: Dial Books.

Philbrick, Rodman. 1993. *Freak the Mighty*. New York: Scholastic.

Ryan, Pam Munoz. 2000. *Esperanza Rising*. New York: Scholastic.

———. 1998. *Riding Freedom*. New York: Scholastic.

Rylant, Cynthia. 1992. *Missing May*. New York: Orchard.

Sachar, Louis. 1998. *Holes*. New York: Farrar, Straus and Giroux.

Soto, Gary. 1991. *Taking Sides*. San Diego: Harcourt Brace Jovanovich.

Spinelli, Jerry. 2002. *Loser*. New York: HarperCollins.

———. 1997. *Wringer*. New York: HarperCollins.

Taylor, Mildred. 2001. *The Land*. New York: Penguin Putnam.

———. 1976. *Roll of Thunder, Hear My Cry*. New York: Dial Books.

Whelan, Gloria. 2000. *Homeless Bird*. New York: HarperCollins.

Woodson, Jacqueline. 1990. *Last Summer with Maizon*. New York: Delacorte.

———. 2000. *Miracle's Boys*. New York: G. P. Putnam's Sons.